THE WRITERS CONQUEST:

ESTABLISH A BRAND

THE WRITERS CONQUEST:

ESTABLISH A BRAND

THOMAS A. FOWLER

THE WRITER'S CONQUEST – ESTABLISH A BRAND.
Copyright © 2016 by Thomas A. Fowler.

To continue the journey, head to WritersConquest.com

ISBN 10: 0-997-3499-1-3
ISBN 13: 978-0-9973499-1-7

Edited by Vivian Trask

Proofread by Bree Crowder

Cover Designed by Harry Forehand III

Formatted by Quincy J. Allen

DEDICATION

This book is dedicated to the Colorado advertising community. The Writer's Conquest is a culmination of lessons learned at Regis University, NEXT Creatives, AdClub, Ad2 Denver and the astonishing talent this state generates. Most importantly, thank you to the incredible agency I've called home, Vladimir Jones. The advertising industry is both unique and insane. I love every minute of it because of the group of co-workers who trudge through the fast turnarounds and creative challenges we face day-to-day as a team.

CONTENTS

THE STRUCTURE

This isn't a book on theory; it is work. Too many books on marketing and author platforms are all talk. They give you ideas, but nothing is put into action. The Writer's Conquest is about logging in hard hours and late nights to become an expert in what you do. The end of every chapter has tangible questions to help you create your brand. At the end of each exercise is a blank page. This is your workspace. This book should not be clean by the end of your reading, but riddled with sketches, tag lines and concepts. Let your brand come to life by learning and doing. Nothing teaches like action.

Let's get to work.

IT'S ALL ON YOU

Your writing can be of great comfort to readers. Your books can have a consistent presence in a person's life. If you have a hard time believing that, think of your favorite author. Their collective works adorn your shelves. They've established their brand. Through either a series or individual works with a shared theme, their writing helped to define a portion of your life. Many great authors start with their brand in place, even if they don't realize it. They merely write the works they want to read, and their brand naturally emerges as their career progresses.

At some point, that author had to sell their writing to a publisher or agent, or both. If the successful author was self-published, they sold their authorship thousands of times via social media, convention appearances and signings. No author worth their salt left their brand unnoticed. They honed their craft, channeled their message and fulfilled an emotional want or need within the industry. They wrote the series no one had seen yet. They reached out to readers and gave them a lasting cathartic experience.

That will be your challenge. How do you make your writing successful and sellable? Find both short and long-term goals to reach out to industry professionals and fans. Those goals will help to create a sustainable business model. This model will be something you believe in because it is based on you and what you love to write. It makes no sense to build a foundation on anything else. That belief will turn into conveyed passion in your messaging. That messaging will lead to conversions. Conversions end the hobby and result in a career. When a brand is successful, it articulates its purpose with immense clarity.

A good brand tells you exactly what it provides. It won't be the right fit for every single consumer in the marketplace—that's an impossible pipe dream—but a focused brand finds the right type of consumer and celebrates them. In order to become a champion of your own making, you have to embrace four major ideas. If you adhere to these four edicts, your brand will be both strong and something you believe in. Put these edicts on a cork board, put sticky notes on the wall, commit them to memory. Frame these four edicts. Keeping them near where you write will keep your priorities straight.

The first edict of The Writer's Conquest: write what you want to read. Nothing helps a brand shine like doing what you love. Little else needs to be said. Think of movies you go to see; you can tell when the cast, the director, and everyone else involved in the making of the film put every effort into making the movie the best it can be. As shown in press junkets, they have a true passion for the film. They share fun stories of late nights to make the movie work, how meticulous the wardrobe department worked to have costume details fit a character.

In the writing world, there are authors who absorb their genre wholeheartedly. This shows in the best way possible. When an author becomes a champion for their genre, it's not by complete accident. They've written a book they wanted to read within their favorite genre. They are equal parts fan and contributor.

Reversely, you can tell when a business tries to enter a market they don't fully understand or have the wherewithal to be an expert in. Embrace the books you love. You feel compelled to write for a particular genre. To go against that to try to accommodate a temporary trend in publishing will show, and it will show in the worst way possible.

The second mantra: write first and write a lot. Agents and editors will dismiss a query without a completed manuscript. Imagine going to a restaurant where the chefs have never actually cooked a meal. It may be delicious, it could taste deplorable. As a result, you'll eat at another restaurant. This is the exact reason your query will be ignored in the slush pile. Writing will also help support your brand because the more you write, the more visibility you'll have—you'll have more to sell.

The third edict: market second. This feeds into the previous two edicts, but is equally important to emphasize. If you fixate on marketing too much, you will forget the core product of your brand: the writing. You are a writer. Write first. It is the single most important element to your brand. Marketing is a priority, but is secondary to writing.

The fourth and final edict: it is your book, your brand. Most companies will carry on if a CEO departs, as they'll just elect a new one. This will not be true of your brand. It is dependent upon you; it lives and dies with your ownership. The weight of that responsibility is strong. Choosing to become a writer is a hard decision to begin with, if you're taking it seriously.

Many believe you write one genius book and the world comes to celebrate you. Those who have done the true work know that is extremely unlikely. The real success stories belong to those who write after they've worked a 9-5 to support their monthly expenses. The real writers are the ones at conventions, meeting fans—talking, interacting, participating on social media, putting in the time it actually takes.

This means you are responsible for the image and likeness of your brand. Granted, depending on your chosen route, there may be agents and publishers to advocate for, and guide, your path. However, the ownership starts and ends with you. You'll also have to make the decision about whether you'll go the traditional or independent route, or do a mix of each. You can ultimately turn down a publishing contract if it isn't the right fit. To go the traditional route, you'll need to find an agent or publisher to represent you. It's up to you to find the right fit. It's also up to you to sell your product. It's no easy feat. However, if you write what you love to read, you write a lot, and you take ownership of your book and your brand, you will successfully establish your brand.

1. **WRITE WHAT YOU WANT TO READ.**

2. **WRITE FIRST. WRITE A LOT.**

3. **MARKET SECOND.**

4. **IT'S YOUR BOOK; IT'S YOUR BRAND.**

EXERCISE ONE

Without doing any marketing research, fill out the following questions. If you don't know the answer, guess. This is a blind test to see what you know already, and what you need to learn. These early questions are vital to channel the focus of your brand. These also need to be honest and more spontaneous. These are the emotional elements that should already be in place in your life. As a result, it's important to be honest. Nothing sticks out like false advertising. Don't be the fast food restaurant trying to sell "artisanal sandwiches."

1. Name your 5 favorite books.
2. Name 5 books you despise.
3. Name your favorite genre(s).
4. What genre(s) do you avoid?
5. How often do you write? Be honest. (every day, twice a week, no consistency)
6. When you write, how many words do you average per hour? If you haven't tested this, give it a try. Don't stare at the timer, though. Just write, and in an hour see what you've done. There are best-selling authors who can barely get 500 words out in a day; there are others who get 6,000-10,000. There isn't a right answer.
7. When people read your books, provide 5 emotional words they'll associate with your book(s).
8. When people think of you, the writer/author, what 5 words will they use to describe you?
9. If you could pick a company that had a brand approach close to what you want for yourself, which company is that?
10. What elements of that company's brand fit you?

WORKSPACE

WORKSHEET

A HARSH TRUTH

The vast majority of advertising is garbage. Think of the last advertisement you saw on the web. You're likely not going to remember. You may recall the most recent advertisement you liked, but there's a reason you can't remember the exact ad or brand. It is because most advertising does not resonate. Many fall into broad categories, groups of ad types that you'll recognize and see all over the place. Here are nine types of advertisements you see all the time:

1. <u>Trends:</u> They're the advertisements chockfull of buzzwords and copycats. When you're driving to work, you see a couple of billboards. You aren't sure if they're for the same company, but they look the same. The next day, if you care, you take notice to see if it was, in fact, the same company. It wasn't. This happens all the time. One company does an incredible job—an agency captures a great moment in which their advertising is not garbage. Then the rest of the competition tries to replicate this success.

This is the reason "craftsmen" and "artisans" were completely exhausted advertising words not long ago. Every company, including fast food restaurants, tried to sell their products as if artisans made them. These test kitchen recipes may have been made by actual artisans in a test kitchen, but they aren't in every restaurant. College students working the late shift part-time aren't artisans. Just as you shouldn't write for a trend, a brand and marketing approach shouldn't cater to trends. Your product should stand alone. If you cater to a trend, you'll either be lost in the shuffle or be considered a copycat. Neither of which are labels you want on your brand.

2. Polish the Turd: For some brands, there comes a point when consumers are so irate with a brand, they want nothing to do with it. There are times when some service providers have lower favorability rankings than others. They own dissatis-faction singlehandedly. Some companies are so large that they don't have to do a thing, and other times the company will rebrand. Things have changed, they promise. An example from the publishing world: when self-published authors heavily revise their work after they've initially published it.

3. "Isn't this funny? By the way, we sell something." Several advertisement approaches are little more than sketch comedy pieces with a fibrously thin connection to the product. A comedy writer creates a concept and then they force a closing statement that connects the skit to the brand or product. A lot of times, the comedy is forced because they refuse to get serious. Comedy works in advertising, but if the consumer can't remember what it was for, the ad failed. In writing, this comes when an author uses social media as a platform for entertainment and forgets to

promote their materials. If the consumer doesn't know what they're buying, why bother?

4. "Why aren't you this celebrity?" The advertisement creates this idealistic moment or life, from the perspective of a celebrity or someone whose life is inexplicably "that incredible." The advertisement makes you covet that life. If you don't have it, others will and then your life will consequently be subpar by comparison. It drives an incredible sense of desire in consumerism. Many authors can do this who have the coveted job of writing fiction. It is an aspiration many hold, but never achieve. Their books are being optioned for film deals, they're writing their next book while sailing the world. If the advertisements fulfill the coveted life, people will indulge.

5. Cheap & Local: The old adage is "you have to spend money to make money." Nothing stands out in advertising quite like cutting corners. Cheap advertising looks cheap; it stands out like an unedited manuscript.

6. "Live your life." These advertisements try to convince you that they're the product that will make every last aspiration you have come true. Have a bucket list? You need this car to drive to every event. Eating unhealthy? Try this one thing and your body will become whatever you need it to be. They pander to an emotional need or want. It is the book you never knew you needed which will fulfill the gaping hole in your life.

7. "Party Up In Here!" What are you doing looking at this advertisement? This beer is having the best party you've ever seen, and you're not at it. Quick, go buy the thing. Your life will be better for it. Go! There are an indiscernible number of beautiful people over here.

Another variation of the life fulfilled, writing has the ability to put you in the shoes of a character you wish you could be. This is why spy novels are so successful, or those of people with lavish lifestyles. It's a coveted method of living, and a book can get you vicariously there.

8. <u>Overindulgence:</u> There's something about just going for it. Every now and then, it can be a great break to get a large burger with cheesy fries. However, these advertisements present the notion that you should do this all the time. That, or you should get the super-charged turbo fueled engine with an in-dash navigation system. The vehicle is a step away from being an automated assistant. The advertisement wants you to think this is acceptable; that having those excessive combo meals won't slow your heart. The introductory level of that truck will get you there just as efficiently as the one with all the add-ons. Your indulgence is their profit.

Not every book sold is a literary classic. There are some books people need to simply get away. They need grand adventure, exotic locations, or mass carnage after a stressful day.

9. <u>We're the Experts:</u> If it's true, then it's effective. You can tell when someone knows what they're talking about, that they've spent years honing whatever it is they're selling. You can also tell when a company executive was selected to be the advocate. They aren't the ones doing the real work. They try to convince you their product is the right one to buy. This is an attempt at justification after two rival companies have already launched. The truth is that they're likely scared they're too late or regretful they didn't come up with the product before their

competition. This book would fall flat pretty quickly without a marketing background.

EXERCISE TWO

1. Name three advertisements you really didn't like, and what specifically you didn't like about them.
2. Which of the 9 types of cliché advertisement categories did these ads fall under?
3. Find an advertisement for a book or author in your genre that you do not like. What was the advertisement medium and what specifically didn't you like? (The writing community is small, don't speak ill of the book or author publicly.)
4. Which of the 9 cliché advertisement approaches does this advertisement fall under?

WORKSPACE

WHEN A BRAND WORKS

Y ou've found the bad. Your eyes and ears have endured the pain. Now, the time has come to look at what does work. A strong, supported brand fulfills one of two things: a want or need. This is an advertising basic principle. A grocery store or transportation system in a busy city fulfills a need. The proprietors of these stores and systems also have to make you *want* to use their service. There are multiple grocery stores, convenience stores, and restaurants. It is up to the brand to make you, the consumer, want to use them to fulfill said need. This is why they use promotions for specific products, offer bundled pricing when you buy more, and have created gas discounts for using their grocery store exclusively. The advertisement approach takes a need, but gives you a reason to want to go to their location. It is a consistent solution with a proven track record.

A fast food restaurant aims less at need and more at want. When you go out to eat, you're paying for the labor of someone else preparing food for you. Take a moment and think of the restaurant you frequent the most. On that menu, you likely choose the same thing most times. The one time you didn't order it, you wished you had. The next time you went, you didn't even look at the menu, but chose your regular. That feeling of comfort was not coincidence, it was branding.

Restaurants, especially fast food, capitalize on the three most tantalizing things humans crave: fat, flavor, and sugar. It's why combo meals have a meaty core item like a burger or sandwich, a salty side item like fries, and a sweet drink to wash it down. Your senses are activated and heightened. Menu testing and design is a part of a brand. Higher end restaurants have to provide fresh options and ingredients not found in the common dining experience. Health food locations need to vet their food suppliers with care to ensure their brand remains valid to the educated consumer. Fast food has to provide comforting food at a convenient pace and low price. Each serves its purpose for various people and various events.

Serving that specific purpose is what goes into strong branding. If you try to please everyone, you'll please no one. A gourmet restaurant won't serve chicken fingers, and fast food joints won't offer sea scallops with a handmade mango chutney. A good author knows the audience they're trying to reach. A great author knows the audience they cannot reach. You won't see a literary poet at a science fiction and fantasy convention. You won't see a horror author with a warm approach to their advertising, unless the approach is deliberately subversive. As much as you'd love to have your books read by millions of readers from every genre, it's not going to happen.

A strong brand knows its purpose. As a result, the nine clichés of bad advertising also have their counterpoints:

1. Create the Trend: The best advertising is not unlike a book that changes the industry. Rather than following a trend, it creates one.

2. Own the Brand: Quality work reaches the right target audience. A company never has to worry about rebranding if everyone supports and embraces the brand.

3. Funny, but also Connected: The best advertisements with humor find a way to also make it about the product. When the connection is made that relates to audiences, that elevates the advertising. It isn't just a comedy sketch that forces a sale; the humor involves the consumer *and* the product.

4. Come Join Me: Rather than show elitism about the brand with a lavish celebrity lifestyle, a brand can succeed by making the life accessible. The right advertisements don't just put the celebrity on a pedestal, they share the luxury with the consumer in an achievable manner.

5. Local and Well Executed: Brands that become advocates for a local community, and take the time to create quality advertising, can develop an incredible following. Locals can be your biggest advocates. When outsiders visit, the local passion translates.

6. Live Your Life: Life can be lived any way you want, but the product helps for a specific reason. That's the right way to speak to the consumer. Help the consumer fulfill the lifestyle they enjoy, rather than try to force them into another way of living. Your brand is a key to opening the door to the life they already have, but can embrace in a different manor.

7. "The party needs you!" That opportunity to engage brings the consumer over to your brand because their life is better having embraced it.

8. <u>Celebration:</u> The advertising is a display of the wonderful events only made better by a product. It's not overindulgence, it's celebratory.

9. <u>We're the Actual Experts:</u> It's not bragging if you back it up. When a brand is the coveted frontrunner of the market, it shows. Consumers are loyal to the brand because it is reliable. They know what they're getting every time they engage the brand, or get a new product. It is the best because the brand is the best.

10. You'll have to know what type of advertising will suit your brand best. Once you decide that, march confidently forward because great advertising resonates. It's why some commercials that aired 30 years ago are still discussed. The advertising knew the brand, and knew the consumer. Most importantly, the advertising brought consumers to the brand in a creative, intelligent way.

EXERCISE THREE

1. Name three advertisements you loved, and what specifically appealed to you.

2. Which of the nine right types of advertisements did these ads fall under?

3. Find an advertisement for a book or author in your genre that you wish you'd made. What was the advertisement medium and what specifically did you love? (The writing community is small, applaud the book and author publicly.)

4. Which of the nine right advertisement approaches does this advertisement fall under?

WORKSPACE

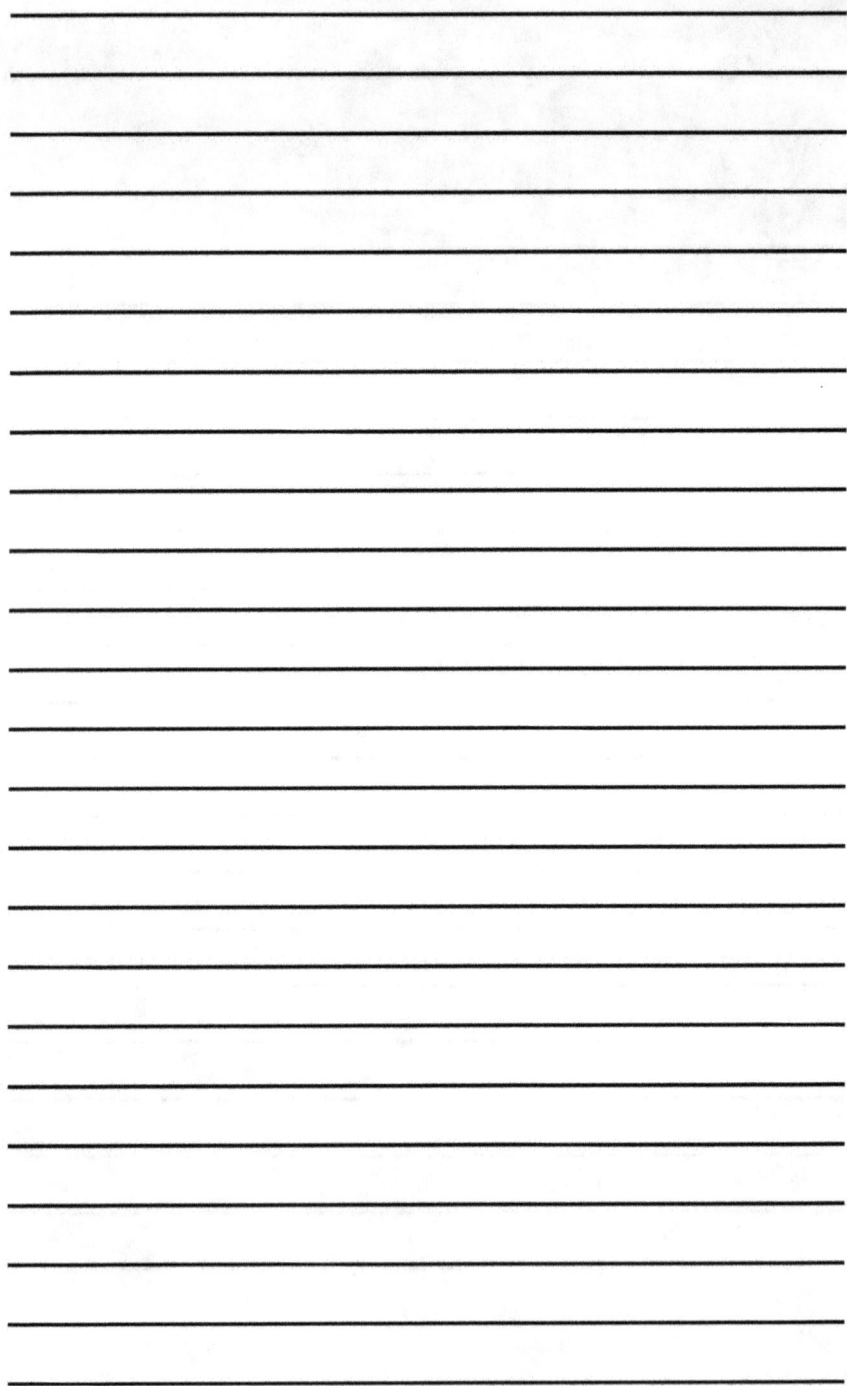

BRAND RESEARCH

T he first step to a good brand is research. The second step is better research. The third step is refining the research to an actionable place. The most intelligent brands are ones that understand at least one of these two things: the niche fulfilled by the brand product, or the untapped area of the market open for the taking. Two anagrams will focus the research, finding the crucial elements needed to create a foundation: S.W.O.T. the P.E.S.T. This foundation will build your brand.

S.W.O.T. focuses on you, the author, and your brand. You'll look in depth at strengths, weaknesses, opportunities, and threats. This will also identify areas where you can take charge of the brand yourself, and where external assistance will be required. P.E.S.T. is an analysis of the marketplace you're entering. The political, economic, social, and technological status of the publishing industry can directly influence your brand and your marketing. Understanding the climate you're selling in is vital to understanding your product message. How you position yourself in certain environments can be the key between awareness and engagement. It is vital that consumers *engage* the brand.

Imagine your dream house. In this scenario money is no object and region is not a factor either. You're likely seeing your dream décor. Here's what people don't think about in the dream scenario: the foundation. How is your house held strong against the elements?

You want to be at the top of bestseller lists with movie deals and the ability to write whatever you feel compelled to as the muse sounds its call. That's the dream home of every author. Research is the foundation of your brand. Without strong framing and precisely formed concrete, the rest of the house's structure doesn't matter because you've already got problems. You can know what counters you want in the kitchen, or what movie posters you want in the theater room, but it will be all for naught if there's shoddy electrical work.

EXERCISE FOUR

1. What is your dream ending (what are some key points in time when your writing career will be deemed a success)? These should be factors only you control.

2. What are some other dream endings that may be out of your control (will require someone else in order to achieve them)? These are events that are not in your control, per se.

WORKSPACE

STRENGTHS

What are your strengths? First, list the ones you possess as a writer. Different authors are known for their particular abilities. Whether it is a knack for world building or creating flawed and beautiful characters, those are elements people will discuss as their favorite pieces when reading your work. It's important to list these because certain readers look for specific experiences. There are those who want tense action, leaving other elements aside in order to move through an intense narrative. Others need a sense of breaking down a moment.

As you read the successful authors in your genre, what are their strengths? Do you share common abilities? If not, that may be a good thing, because you may have a specialty the market is in need of. However, if you are able to embrace tropes you see in your favorite authors' work, you will likely be able to sell to publishers, agents and consumers in that same market. Connecting through a common thread may be the path needed for publication.

What are your strengths beyond writing? If you have a background in art or graphic design, write it down. If you're charismatic and can work a crowd, log it. These expanded capabilities will help you support your core product (your writing). Incredible coding skills means an author website will be a breeze. A background in English education means your grammatical knowledge can tie into proof-reading income on the side.

You can utilize these secondary strengths in your brand and marketing. You don't have to know how to build a website, you don't have to know how to design a cover, but you do have to know where your strengths are best used. A good speaker can give lectures and speeches to raise awareness of your product and your author brand. A good listener can interview fellow authors and post those interviews on your blog or website. This can create a network of support to promote your work when the time comes for your book to hit the shelves.

These strengths will play a part when you create your brand strategy. For now, create a list of strengths you possess.

EXERCISE FIVE

1. List three strengths you have as a writer.
2. List additional strengths you possess beyond writing that could support your marketing efforts.

WORKSPACE

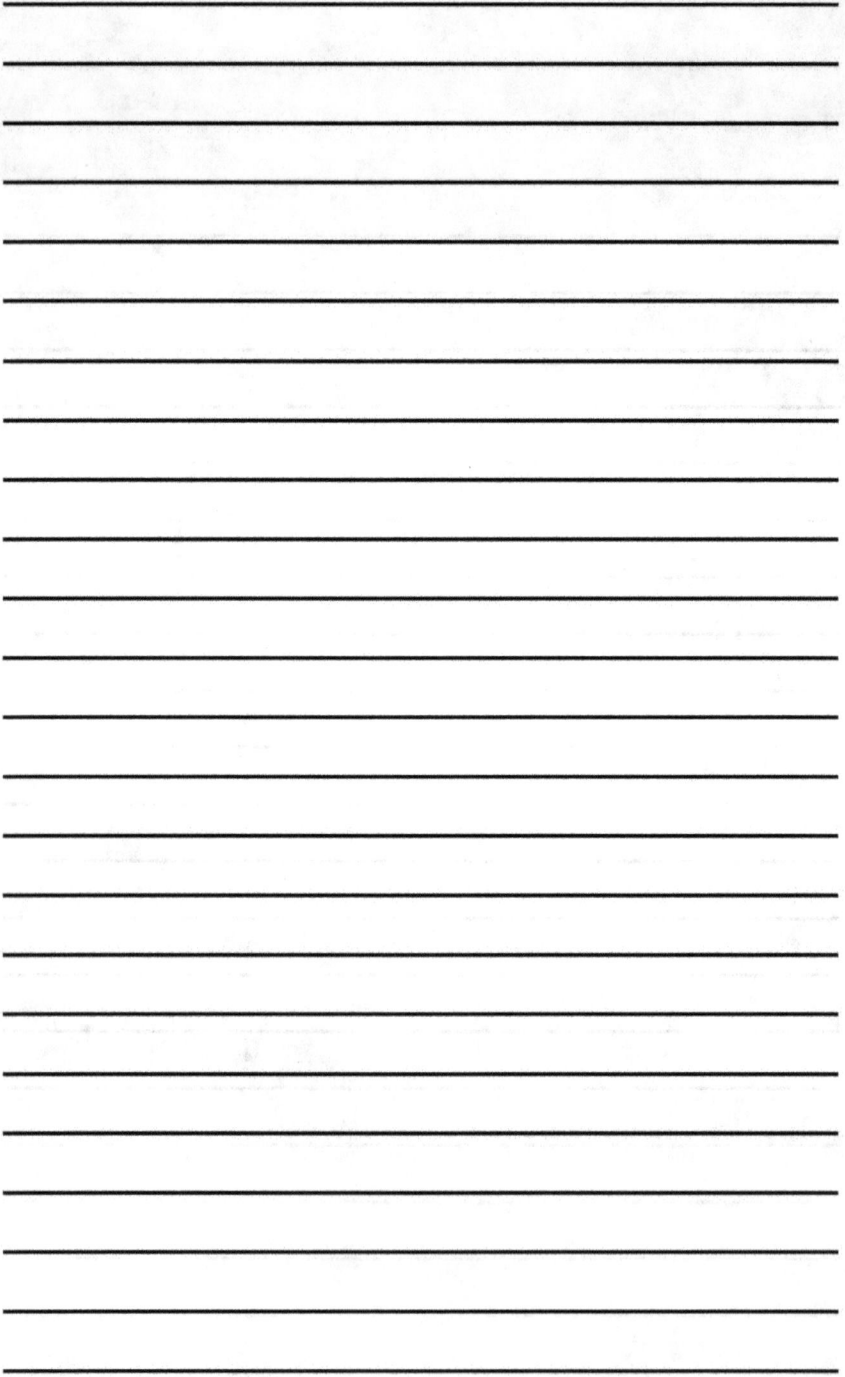

WEAKNESSES

For all the strengths you were told you possess as a writer, your critique group and beta readers surely came back with criticism. If they didn't, find a new critique group and stop using your sister as a beta reader. As a writer, what are your weaknesses? Are you tangled in sentence structure? Does passive voice persistently reveal itself in your pages? You're not a perfect writer; be honest and admit where you need improvement.

Consequently, you also have to divulge what your weaknesses are outside of writing. Are you ill tempered? Do you compare public speaking to the emotional equivalent of getting dental work without anesthesia? Again, don't worry about what these mean for now. This is the research phase. You are mapping out what you know. It's pivotal because certain elements of your writing, marketing, and approach may reveal itself from this research.

Don't feel nervous about putting something down. If you've been told your settings are indiscernible or your dialogue sounds like toddlers screaming, remember writing is a never-ending learning process. You'll address, and face, these weaknesses. That's how you learn. The more honest you are about this, the easier the rest of this brand establishment will become. If you disillusion yourself into thinking you have a great eye for design, when in reality your working experience involves clip art and the Comic Sans font, this is going to be really hard to get through. Create two separate lists to determine what your weaknesses are as a writer, and secondary areas of skill sets.

EXERCISE SIX

1. List three weaknesses you have as a writer.
2. List additional weaknesses you possess beyond writing that could affect your marketing efforts.

WORKSPACE

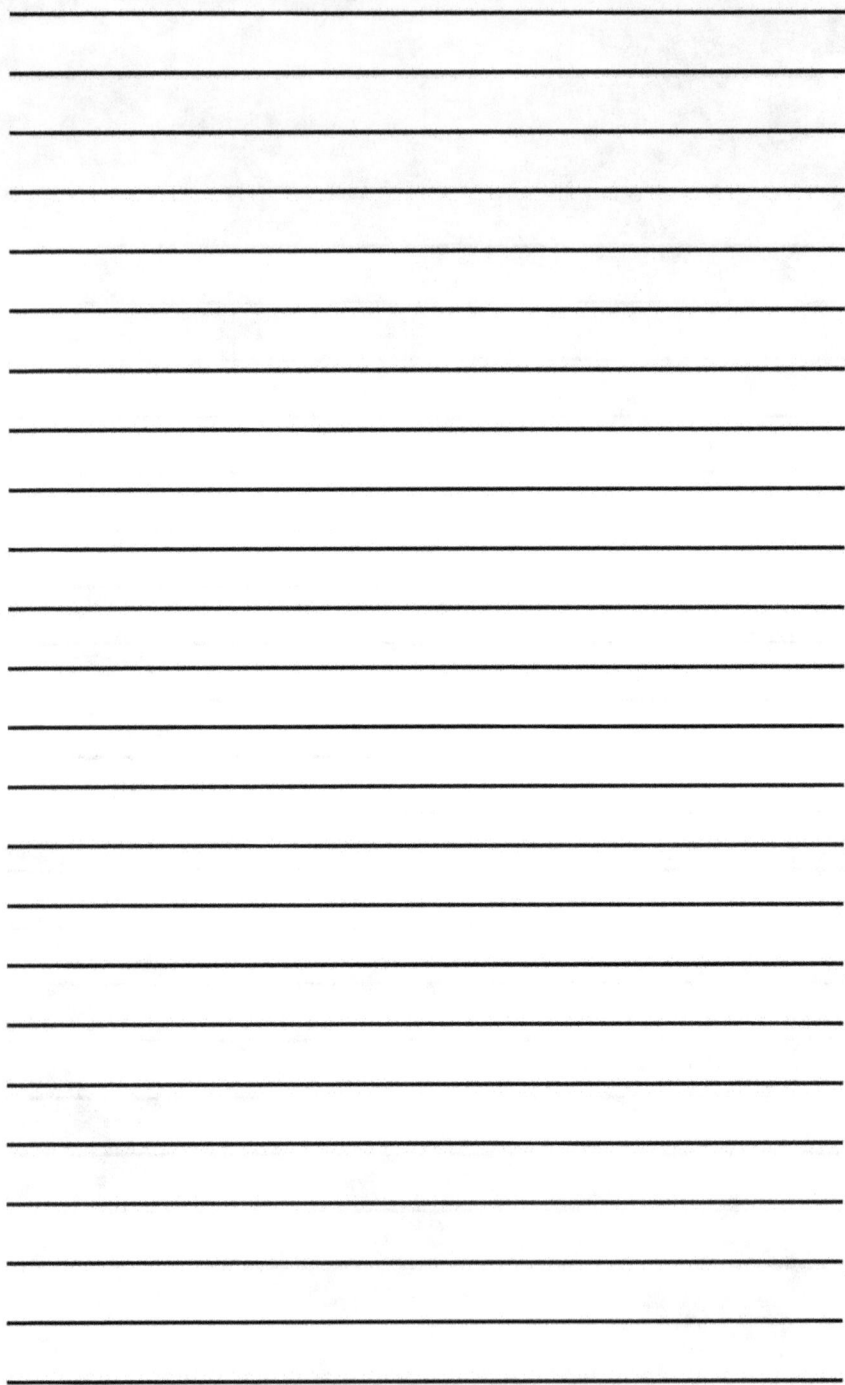

OPPORTUNITIES

T he last elements of S.W.O.T. are opportunities and threats. They hone in on the current market, and specifically what's occurring in your genre, with fellow authors and the industry as a whole. Take on more research in this category than most. Strengths and weaknesses asked you to take an honest look at yourself. The challenge now is to understand not just what you can do, but what others are doing and how you can capitalize on what isn't being done. Now it's time to take an honest look at the competition.

As self-publishing has seen a surge and technology provides new challenges to contract negotiations, it's important to look for the opportunity in the industry. eBooks are offering new elements to the reading process with heightened interactivity. Simultaneously, traditionally printed books are far from dead. Despite the click-bait headlines stating that "Print is dead!" or that the industry is headed for an inevitable graveyard, that is actually far from true. There is a strong market for traditional print, and despite tablet sales plateauing, eBook sales are still a strong market for wider variety.

With the multitude of platforms for publishing, and ease of getting product into the market, comes saturation. This saturation means more books are being published. With over-saturation comes a harder threshold to cross to audiences. Convincing consumers your product is either unique or high quality is now a heightened challenge. Self-published works struggle immensely with image perception. Additionally, with traditional publishers, price drops in the digital market cause a conflict in pricing. Too high pricing and the sales aren't there; too low pricing and the product is perceived as low value. Even offering an eBook for free tarnishes the image of the author brand. If it's free, it can't be that good.

Herein lies your challenge: what is the opportunity for your brand to separate itself in the market? Is your author brand based on a long-running series that aims to build loyalty, or will your brand be better known for a strong technological embrace? This is where guidance can only take you so far. There come moments in time when you have to make a decision. If you want to create highly interactive eBooks, start learning everything you can about the technology.

The opportunity section means you have to see what is being published. You are seeing what is being done with eReaders and tablets. You are also focusing on traditional outlets that are still successful. The key, no matter what opportunity you approach, is brand differentiation. Brand differentiation is the specific approach to your marketing, as a whole, that allows your brand to stand out from the rest.

Visit your grocery aisle and notice the brand packaging of different cereals. How does the packaging look for the big named kid's cereals? What are the colors? Design choices? Does one brand of cereal manufacturers use more cartoon characters than the other? What about the organic cereals? Notice the more earth-toned color palette as opposed to the Saturday morning cartoon approach. What does the organic brand of cereal promote over the sugary goodness? They're both great. However, they aim to fulfill varied needs for the consumer.

This is the reason that some readers go from graphic novels to science-fiction epics, or from the memoir of a female comedian to a legal thriller: they're different experiences for a reader.

That's what the other book is there to do. It capitalizes on a different opportunity. If your writing is meant to entertain, that's great; it fulfills that purpose and want in a reader. Simultaneously, if you're writing for a specific niche audience, you should expect there to be less cross-promotional opportunity and audience discovery. Instead, it becomes pivotal to hit your target niche with remarkable precision.

Making the right decision about what your authorship fulfills will let you know what kind of author you want to be to your readers. Are you that awesome piece of nostalgia to embrace while wearing pajamas on a weekend, or are you the author that encourages a better way of thinking about life? Are you trying to bring to light a healthier way of living? When you know the unique sell readers will identify your author brand with, you can market to that identity. Therein lies one of the greatest challenges for your author brand: identifying your opportunity.

Find an author who is known for religious thrillers that provides an alternate take on history. Now ask a few people who they think that author might be. If there were at least two answers that were the same, that's a branded author. Try a similar exercise for epic fantasy, or identify an author who writes strong romantic drama. When one author is associated with something specific by multiple readers, they've done their job in identifying the opportunity.

The branding can be extremely specific or broad. The key is that you are providing an opportunity to readers. If someone has written your novel concept already, how will you separate the work? You may think that you haven't identified your opportunity yet. You may just be writing the book you can't find on shelves, which is smart.

That's your opportunity. There's a reason that book hasn't been published yet. Either another author hasn't been able to sell the notion of the book yet, or you have created a unique experience for the reader.

Opportunity can be experience too. Is there an experience you're wanting from a book, or author, but haven't seen yet? Is there a spin on traditional horror tropes within your novel, separating it from those writing in the traditional methods of the genre? There's another opportunity. Remember, it's your book; it's your brand. The opportunity is yours to identify.

Think of it like your elevator pitch: the briefest sell of your book. This condensed sell ensures your book's concept is honed and crafted. It is also a concise selling tool to get to a quick conversion. Imagine you're at a writing conference, and your ideal agent is there. They're taking pitch sessions, but they're limited to 5 minutes.

You'd better have a lightning elevator pitch ready. If you can't explain the book with a unique hook that sells fast, the idea isn't refined enough. Agents won't read hundreds of pages of your manuscript if the basic concept cannot be articulated. Their livelihood depends on selling the concept to publishers. Therefore, if you cannot sell it, how can they?

Your brand and marketing opportunity should be equally concise. If you're trying to sell your author website or social media accounts for more followers, how will you sell anything if you can't explain who you are in the time it takes to ride an elevator? Next time you need an elevator ride, pitch your author brand or book to a stranger. See if they understand and want to buy. If not, refine until the opportunity reveals itself.

The reason encouragement lives so prominently is because everyone wants the next big thing. Publishing industry advances occur when the next great book series or technological advancement occurs.

The newest line of tablets provides an additional chance for further interaction with the reader. One reason you shouldn't write for a trend is that the second YA vampire romance became popular, submissions became oversaturated. Suddenly a specific genre became white noise. Publishers are more interested in finding the next trend. Create that trend by clearly identifying your brand opportunity.

EXERCISE SEVEN

1. What did your three favorite authors do that gave them their publishing opportunity?
2. What did those authors write that established their brand?
3. What opportunities arise if you go the traditional publishing route?
4. What opportunities arise if you go the self-publishing route?
5. What opportunities reside within your genre that haven't been done yet?
6. What have authors in your genre done that proved a unique opportunity for either author awareness or increasing sales?
7. What have authors in your genre not done yet?

WORKSPACE

THREATS

T
he first thing the publishing industry does well is encourage. One opportunity publishing offers is creative collaboration and encouragement. There are few in this industry who want someone to fail. When you receive a rejection from an agent or publisher, you shouldn't feel like you should "give up" or that "this is garbage." It is one rejection from one person based on their opinion. Encouragement thrives in the publishing industry because when more people talk about books, the industry gets better.

The second thing the publishing industry does well is collaborate. Encouragement and collaboration aren't far apart. However, the distinction must be noted. Some will say "Good job, go for it." Others will go further and help edit, even co-write. If you haven't gone to conferences or a critique group yet, then you're in for a pleasant experience. From agents, publishers, and fellow authors, everyone helps each other. As a result, when I tell you this section titled "Threats" is an assessment of competition, the word must be filtered.

In marketing and advertising, the threats area is where you find out who has market share above you. Fierce competition begins to gain hold of market share percentages. You should not do this with publishing. It will turn against you. The collaborative atmosphere means your assessment of threats should not become a vocal, or identifiable, area of your marketing. Rather, it's a healthy assessment of books and authors that you'll be compared to. In that assessment, you can decide how you can separate yourself from that comparison so your work is not perceived as derivative. The acronym from business classes is S.W.O.T., not S.W.O.C. (that 'c' for competition isn't there for a reason).

The truth of the matter is that the publishing industry doesn't care if you worked years on your book. If the story's been done before, it's been done before. Nothing will change that; someone beat you to the punch. Therefore, you have but a few choices: revise to give it a unique spin, or work on something else. A brutal truth, but the truth nonetheless. It is your job to separate yourself in the market.

Threats exist in the marketplace. A smart marketer understands the threats and knows how to adapt accordingly. Smartphone manu-facturers understand who dominates market share. They also know what they can offer and where they can address a threat. Some people need the latest smartphone with a tablet-sized screen, others just need a phone. Companies make strategic decisions based on which threats they're addressing. Your author brand has to do the same.

Identify your threats. What are the books you'll be compared to? More importantly, how can you work your narrative to ensure there is no way an agent, publisher, or reader would consider your work derivative? It's okay if your topic has been done, and it's even okay if it's close to something that's been recently published. However, the work has to be your own. In addition, it has to be sold as your own.

There are four categories to understand additional threats and opportunities, and that's where the next half of your research comes into play.

EXERCISE EIGHT

1. What are five books your work will be compared to?
2. What similarities does each of the five books have with your narrative?
3. How can your approach separate your novel from these books?
4. What authors will you be compared to?
5. What marketing efforts have they done that, if you used the same approach, would appear derivative?
6. What marketing efforts have these authors not done?

WORKSPACE

POLITICAL

Y ou've looked at yourself; now gauge the environment your book is entering. How politics can influence a book release may be hard to gauge, especially in fiction. However, without an understanding of your surroundings, your marketing could end up far removed from your target audience. Using politics for passionate storytelling and characters can push a narrative and create an author platform that excites readers.

Specific events can alter your political perspective. A harrowing tragedy often results in movies with related incidents within the narrative being delayed, or editing in post-production to remove the content from being associated with the tragedy. Politics can have a direct impact on your creative work. With today's environment, events are shared in real time. As a result, you have to assess the politics of the current atmosphere. This will allow you to understand if there are elements of your book that may need to be edited or addressed to accommodate the public to avoid insensitive perception.

Sensitive content in your book can be an incredible starting point for intellectual discussion. However, insensitive use of a political environment can cause backlash from your readers. If you include a political hot button topic for the sake of shock value or trying to sell more books, it will catch on with the consumer. Political topics have an incredible ability to divide readers, and can be used strategically for your readership.

You can decide to have your protagonist make a political stand. There's nothing wrong with that, and decisive characters that stand their ground make for great conflict. Making such a stand in your primary characters does one thing though: entrench the narrative in a political environment. The consequent discussion can create conversation and raise awareness. On the other side, expect the opposite reaction. Those in opposition of your political views will speak against your product. Your author brand will begin establishing loyalists and protesters.

If you make such a decision, the marketing approach will have to be equally thought out. Do you play it safe and market for the entertainment, allowing the politics to take a backseat, or do you take that head-on and spark social media conversations? Either works, but you have to be ready to embrace that decision. Once that decision is made, altering reader perception will be like turning a frigate on a dime.

When will your book be released? During campaign season, political thrillers are the perfect releases. It's all coming out in the muckraking political ads. If you have a murder mystery taking place in Washington, the timed release of your book could be perfect. A calm read can use marketing as an antithesis of such stressful times. By the time major election seasons end, most people are absolutely sick of the ads, the pandering for votes, and blatant spin on facts to diminish the image of the opposing party. A light comedy set far away from the world of politics can be the simplistic escape of election season that people are looking for.

So, look at the politics of today. Understanding where your book, and you as an author, fit within politics will help inform your marketing decisions. It is but one part of four in the analysis. Also understand that politics with timely publication can catapult a novel into higher relevance than one without any pertinence in present-day society.

It boils down to passion. If politics is a passion of yours, use it. Understand that implementing politics will encourage certain perceptions of your brand. If they are welcome perceptions, then absolutely use that. If not, make the political inferences subtle or scrap them. Write what you want to read. The odds are that you've done enough research to understand what can help create a better narrative without getting atop a soapbox.

EXERCISE NINE

1. Were there any events in the last five years that could be directly compared to your writing?
2. If so, would it be perceived as insensitive should your narrative be published?
3. What political figures do you follow closely, either from the past or present?
4. Do their politics have a place in your narrative?
5. If so, are there politics embedded in the voice of the overall novel, or better suited for a character?
6. Are the political tones, or figures, in your novel typically present within your genre?
7. Will your book cause a political divide with any major party in your market?

8. If so, will your work be strongly viewed by the supporting party, enough so to warrant the alienation of the opposing audience?

WORKSPACE

ECONOMIC

Economic influence on marketing is a topic expansive enough to warrant its own book. When writing your books, you shouldn't concern yourself with economic trends and consumer habits. However, a marketer has to consider the economic environment. Consumers fluctuate their spending habits based on the economy. When times are hard, spending on entertainment can increase significantly. It sounds contradictory, but the reason for this increase is that people are looking for an escape. When consumer confidence is higher, flexible spending on items such as books, movies, and music can be justified with greater ease.

Never let the economy decide when your book is released. There will never be the perfect economic situation for a book to be published. This is because while entertainment consumption goes up during rough economic times, pricing suffers. When people are making less, they want to pay less. The economic circumstances that exist as you begin your marketing may determine your selling price. However, during periods of economic success, consumers are more flexible on discretionary spending. With such periods comes choice;

spending from providers is up, which means more product is available. Thus, your book will have a harder time separating in a more saturated market.

Going the traditional route means your book release date isn't even an option for you. Your publisher will be worrying about pricing and how to reach consumers. In self-publishing, though, pricing can be one of the hardest decisions to make. To have strong profits on printed versions of a book, prices have to be rather high. The price point may be so high that only loyalists will justify purchasing. When publishers or printers see drastic increase in production costs, those have to be offset somehow. That cost then goes into your expenses, and therefore hits the consumer.

The economic environment, again, should not hinder your writing what you want. However, when it comes to creating a marketing plan and strategy, the economy has to be taken into consideration. When house sales are down and jobs aren't growing, how do you create a marketing plan that appeals to a consumer struggling with elementary financial needs? If the average consumer has to decide between purchasing a book or meeting a basic need, the decision is quite easy: it's the hierarchy of need.

A shopper needs a sense of security, food, good health, employment, and many other things before they'll be willing to spend money on your book. Consequently, you have to consider which groups within a specific economy will be willing to make said purchase. Aiming your marketing towards struggling families has little place in entertainment. Sure, everyone loves a relatable narrative about a struggling family. The key is to understand who is consuming the product, and how they're consuming the product. Pricing and value perception will come into play later. For now, research the economy. Understand your reader's financial situation.

EXERCISE TEN

1. Go back to the three authors you mentioned in "Exercise Six." What are the prices of their books, both in print and in digital formats?

2. Check the bestseller lists in your genre. What are their prices for print and digital?

3. For the books you've researched, what elements are in place (such as giveaways or promotional pricing periods)?

4. What challenges could be present with the release of your book, with pricing and economic environment?

5. Because of your chosen path—whether it be traditional, self-published, or a hybrid approach—what economic hurdles will you have to face as a result?

WORKSPACE

SOCIAL

Social environments require delicate navigation. The further technology advances, the more transparent your interactions become. Think of how the face of public scandals have changed in the last 15 years. It was mainly word of mouth and phone calls, a few e-mails too, that raised awareness. That ability will continue to grow as more join social media. Additional platforms provide a variety of ways to share said information. In fact, social media has been responsible for outrages that have been unfounded. After all, it only takes one uneducated social media user to share. Unfortunately, in this day and age, something shared can be construed as instantaneous fact, regardless of factual basis. The usage of headlines that are deemed "Click-bait," (headlines written strategically to invoke emotion, incentivizes users to share) have skyrocketed.

Then there's the opposite side of this coin, when you legitimately bury yourself because of impulsive action. There are a multitude of examples, but the focus will remain on two: one in the writing industry and one that is a general cautionary tale.

Let's say every year an esteemed newspaper publishes their top books of the year; it is a summary of their favorite selections that were also on their bestseller list. To get on either of these is considered an achievement.

So, this author is on the bestseller list and their career is thriving. The esteemed newspaper publishes their favorites of the year and this author is not on it. Most would think, "Oh well, maybe next book or next year." This author went on a social tirade. Social media posts were full of rage and bewilderment as to how this author wasn't included.

None of the results were in the author's favor. Instead, there were two trains of thought. The first argument was that the bestselling list is statistical fact, and she succeeded. "Best of" lists are based on opinion, and therefore out of the author's hands. So, complaining about the personal choice of another human being isn't worth the headache. The second argument was that the author should've taken the win. This author was able to write fiction full-time, an aspiration many hope to achieve and struggle to acquire. This author was on a bestseller list and writing full-time. In both arguments, the author appeared ungrateful and self-involved.

Everyone, from readers to industry professionals, berated this author. When scenarios like this transpire on social media, it doesn't disappear. The Internet holds on to these things forever. If the author has a publicist, they have an uphill battle to undertake. Using the "account was hacked" approach has little influence unless there's something to physically prove the hack occurred. An apology can come after the fact, but many will perceive it as as a disingenuous, forced public relations act of contrition. A tirade has occurred. There is nothing to be done about it except to fess up and try to move forward. It's worth mentioning that in this social environment, there are times when there is no turning back.

Everyone should employ discretion and patience before responding to negative social media posts or articles. The easy way to lay the groundwork is to search the web for the term "restaurant social media tirade." There are plenty of examples, pick whichever you like. Read through and come back.

Done? Good.

So, a citizen went to the restaurant and they weren't happy with the experience. They decided to post something about the restaurant. Then the owner decided to "correct" this criticizing patron. Things escalated and dissolved quickly. In some cases, restaurants were closed within months of said tirade. The amount of attention and eyes on social media grows every day. National news outlets will now cover social media stories. In fact, many of them now have dedicated time for social media interactions. This proves that spoken words are not easily forgotten. Seek out better examples of social media engagement.

The first decent example is no engagement at all. If the post appears as if someone is simply seeking attention, ignore it. There are different types of negative posts. There are those with constructive criticisms, and then there are trolls. Trolls on the Internet are those who don't care what the content is, they're simply seeking attention via the discussion and trying to enrage others. Those are the ones you either don't engage or block, depending on where it's shared and what control you have over the discussion area. Arguing back will only exacerbate the issue(s). If there is someone setting a positive example, thank him or her. Engage them, ignore the haters. Leaving hatred to itself will keep it in its own shadow.

The second type of intelligent social media engagement is constructive discussion. You can turn negative posts into a new fan with smart discussion. This is adequate for times when the person appears to be approachable. If they negatively discussed your book, but they talk about other books they love, talk about those other books. Perhaps you have another book they might like. Sending them a free eBook version might make them appreciative and more likely to look for aspects they like in your narrative. Once your book is with the public, it's up to the public to decide how they feel about your book. It's a psychological challenge to let your work go out into the world, but once it's released, you have to let it go.

Any time you feel the need to start arguing or post about a divisive subject, take a breath. Think about what one post has the ability to do to your brand, your book, and your livelihood. Consequently, think about what the opposite has the ability to do.

To summarize: if you're ever unsure, leave it be.

Now it's time to focus on logistical strategy that isn't troll feeding or angry corrections. The easiest route is looking at your "competition." Again, competition is used in quotation marks because of the collaborative atmosphere of the publishing industry. They are competition in the sense that they have some ownership of the market you look to own. However, getting positive reviews from others in the industry can help you find the right audience. Knowing who's writing in your genre, what's being published, and how those industry professionals are interacting is the research needed to formulate strategy.

Your research needs to be twofold. See what's being done that can be of assistance to you. Nothing looks worse than a company trying to be someone they're not. Have you ever watched a television commercial and thought, "That didn't match up"? The social strategy is trying to be something they're not. Creating humorous, meme-based social media full of cats has no place if you're writing a strong, political drama. Understand what your readers are seeking, and how they're engaging their authors. Are giveaways of books getting strong interaction? What kinds of articles or posts are being commented on or favorited? It can also be a great way to find out who represents your authors if they're using Twitter or Facebook with their agent. Now you know some people to query when you're ready to submit your book, if that's your chosen route.

Then it's important to see what isn't being done; therein resides your main opportunity for differentiation. If you're writing fantasy, and your books contain specific parameters to your created world, post about the research. As you had to look into a particular region, post your interviews. Create a focused theme that can slowly bring in attentive readers that can then be converted into dedicated fans. Are elements of your narrative culled from specialists from an industry? Post the interviews that can tie in toward invitations to sell books to social media users. The social environment can provide engagement with those in your field and those reading the same books that got you hooked on writing in the first place.

EXERCISE ELEVEN

1. Going back to the three authors from "Exercise Six," what are your favorite authors doing on social media?
2. What are they not doing that is a missed opportunity?
3. Look at publishing companies within your genre. What are they doing via social media to engage consumers?
4. More importantly, what social media strategies are they utilizing that translate to sales and pre-orders?
5. What are some social media strategies from companies outside of publishing that you like?
6. How can that be translated to the publishing industry, and more specifically your book and your brand?

WORKSPACE

_____

_____

_____

_____

_____

_____

_____

_____

_____

_____

_____

_____

_____

_____

_____

_____

_____

_____

_____

_____

_____

_____

TECHNOLOGICAL

Here comes a fun portion of research that will be outdated a few minutes after completion. In today's market, technology changes rapidly and you, the aspiring writers and published authors, are unlikely to have inside tracks on future technologies. Therefore, it is important to understand what you can accomplish, and plan on adapting where necessary. As great as it would be to create a website, set up some social media and a blog, and feel like you've done all there is to do, at this point that's "par for the course." You will have to maintain your site, you will have to create consistent content, and you will have to adjust your technological approach to marketing throughout the course of your career. Never forget rule one: write. If you're not writing, then you have no validation to your marketing.

Understand your timeframes and capacity. Understand that customized websites take a very long time and can become very expensive. Website templates exist for a reason. Based on your ability to design and manipulate templates, you can create something that appears custom. At the same time, think of reader perception based on your site. If you have a gorgeous site, with nothing to show for it, you need to write more to sell more. If you have a mediocre site, with little content, publishers and agents may not like that your author platform has a weak and inconsistent presence.

There are some fundamental pieces that have to be put in place if you want to succeed in marketing. Despite what everyone tells you, it's not all digital. The plan should include face-to-face time with other authors and industry professionals, and convention time with fans. Sign some autographs. Never mistake the power of human interaction.

Technology is often mistaken as a substitute for emotion. A gorgeous site means little if it conveys nothing. The correct approach allows technology to evoke the right emotion you seek to provide to your reader. Fulfill a desire or need. That's where your research in what technology to implement should come from, not because a platform checklist demands an author page. What fulfillment does the technology serve?

There are two things technology should fulfill. Again, it boils down to wants and needs. They are two of advertising's fundamental core values. Consumers have wants and needs that must be fulfilled. You, the author, have to take care of that want. How does technology help you convey that emotional need? There is a void in a reader's life. It could be momentary; the want could be looking for a long-term author to commit to. That's why franchises and series work. The emotional need for characters they can know, find comfort in returning to at a moment's notice, provides an emotional comfort for the reader. That's what your writing is capable of accomplishing.

You also have to consider purchasing experiences. What do they want once they decide to buy your book? Ease. Nothing turns off a customer more than not being able to find what they're looking for. Technology is your bridge to help readers, agents and publishers.

This bridge can be short and sturdy, or it can be long and unstable. That's where technology research comes into play. How do you allow your information and marketing to be easy to understand and acquire? When you can deliver the exact product to your consumer without a glitch, that's technology at its finest.

EXERCISE TWELVE

1. What technology are you already familiar with?
2. What technology are you unfamiliar with?
3. Who do you know that could help with the technology, either through transference of knowledge or executing certain aspects for you?
4. How can technology better serve your novel?
5. What needs or wants does your proposed technology fulfill that will help sell your books?
6. Who are three authors you've seen with intelligent digital strategies?
7. What technologies and approaches are they taking?
8. How can you capture that approach and translate it to your author platform and published works?

MAPPING OUT RESEARCH

Now that your initial research period has concluded, what do you do with that research? You've taken the time to gather your strengths, open up about your weaknesses, identify opportunities and assess your threats. In addition, you have a comprehensive understanding of the political, environmental, social and technological environment you, the author, will be entering. These are eight classic assessments in the business world. By knowing these, you have the key to your first portion of research.

Knowing also means you know how to construct your brand. Right now you understand the environment in which your brand resides. The other half of knowing is being able to state how your brand will interact with this environment. Imagine this portion as creating your battle strategy. You aren't ready to invade. Right now, you understand the battlefield but you also have to know your method of attack; where your infantry enters, when air support is appropriate, how naval forces can shell an area before releasing infantry. All elements of your brand invading have to be known before the battle commences.

To prepare, let's summarize the battlefield. Create brief summaries of each of the eight categories in your research. These should be single paragraphs that serve as reminders of the detailed research you've done. That way, you can reference more detail as it becomes necessary. The summaries are the key points of the battlefield. Where is the bridge that will become a choke point, and cut off your forces if lost? Where is the high ground for pivotal defense?

Summarize the exercises you've completed thus far by answering these questions regarding your S.W.O.T. and P.E.S.T. analysis.

EXERCISE THIRTEEN

1. STRENGTH: What is the key strength you possess from a business standpoint, which will be the best tool in creating a marketing plan for your brand? Why?

2. WEAKNESS: What is one weakness that ultimately intimidates you? This is what has been a strong criticism from others or what you fear will be criticized the most in your marketing.

3. OPPORTUNITY: In your genre, what is one thing you haven't seen yet from a marketing standpoint?

4. THREAT: Who are the five authors you consider your strongest competition?

5. POLITICAL: What political subject, being actively discussed in news and social media, has relevancy to your author brand and book subject matter?

6. ECONOMICAL: What trend in the publishing industry alarms you the most in terms of how consumers are purchasing books?

7. SOCIAL: How has social media helped your most comparable author and ideal publisher?

8. TECHNOLOGICAL: What technology will best serve your author brand?

9. Answer these eight questions, and the first major section of your author brand is prepared. Now this will tie in to the "Brand Strategy." It's time to take the research you've found, and start planning your attack.

WORKSPACE

THE BRIEF

The time has come to take your brand research and strategy and begin the process of implementing everything into an actionable plan. This will take several distinct steps. Some of these elements will overlap, and you should go back for revisions. Keep in mind any due dates. After all, if you have a publisher and your marketing is supplementary, it might be a moot point if you start your brand-specific advertising a few weeks after the release.

A creative brief: the first major step in creating your physical plan. The research is over. While the thought that goes into the brief is extensive, the actual physical result shouldn't go any further than five pages. In fact, if it comes out at two pages, you're likely to have a better execution. This means you've broken your brand down to its most basic elements. Think of your book summary: often the best approach to writing a summary is beginning with the one sentence version, then the one paragraph version. Eventually you'll have the single page and five page versions, and this allows you to understand the most elementary pitch of your book.

If you cannot describe your book or your brand in a single sentence, you don't understand the fundamental core of what you're trying to sell. Those simple statements allow your readers to capture the essence of your book and your brand. Those are the two things you own. Now, certain elements of those will be surrendered upon getting an agent or publisher via the traditional route. However, strategic negotiation and strong writing will help ensure your marketing approach and brand are consistent. The nice thing is that as campaigns for your individual books can have variance, your author brand is you. Frankly, if your brand is straying from who you are as a person, you probably need to rethink how you researched. Some people try to market themselves as these dynamic speakers that could moonlight as standup comedians on the side, but in reality they are quiet individuals. It won't work. Embrace who you are, find how your personality connects and resonates with others. Gather your S.W.O.T., put your P.E.S.T. next to you, and keep your Brand Strategy handy. Let the brief begin.

1. Background reasoning is the purpose for your brand to exist. It's not "because I wanted to be a writer." Imagine a restaurant's advertising campaign being "we make food." You have to find reasoning with an emotional core. There is a reason you write the genre and books you write. Perhaps you saw a horror film as a teenager, and that thrilling scare stayed with you. Perhaps your brand stems from a children's book that never left you. A single sentence: What is the reason for your brand to exist?

2. Brand objective. Your personal objective has already been established. However, this is your brand's objective. Is it meant to be informative, entertaining, hopeful? What objective is fulfilled with your writing?

3. Your brand goals are the tangible elements you need to accomplish for your brand to succeed. Book sales, social media followers, newsletter subscribers... what are the goals you need to achieve for the brand to be considered a success?

4. Target demographics include the people who will actually engage with your brand. There are certain people who read science fiction, others who read historical fiction. It's plain and simple that aiming for a retired man in Florida with a YA romance probably isn't going to resonate. If a certain demographic is that outside the norm, they're looking for those books with dedication. They'll find it if you market your brand well enough. Think about the main people who read your genre. That is your demographic. There are also secondary demographics: those who won't be the most obvious choice, but are avid fans of your genre.

5. Your brand tone provides the emotional voice of your brand. Would it best be served with a stoic sense and a strong voice, or is it an empathetic tone from a youthful perspective? How do those choices define your tone?

6. Your brand messaging tells your audience what your brand is trying to say. If the audience is to take away a cautionary tale from your writing, your brand messaging should provide that. If your brand provides sprawling epics about hope living in woeful times, your branding should provide emotional messaging that allows your audience to understand that's what your brand provides.

7. Visuals target a wider group of consumers. After all, audiences find pictures more compelling than words. It's not something you, the author, wants to hear. However, this is marketing.

Visual elements are more compelling in advertising than words. What colors match your brand? Are splattered oil splotches in a broken town helping to convey your apocalyptic tone? Do you need a young couple on the verge of kissing in a meadow with soft matte overlays? How can you visually represent your brand?

8. As your brand enters the market, you'll have to measure the results. How do you plan on measuring your marketing efforts? Website analytics, book sales, number of appearances, increased social media followers... these are all viable options as to what your measurement considerations should be. It's up to what your brand embraces and delivers to the reader.

9. Production parameters will help make sure you can herd the cats. What is your schedule, your budget, what are the exact deliverables you aim to create before you reach your due date?

Write all nine of these elements down; now you have a creative brief. It is a summary of what you will accomplish, by when, and how it is being executed. Most importantly, it is asking why: why your brand is compelling, intriguing, and worthy of investment in monetary purchase and time provision. That is what your brand has to convey the most. With busy lives and not much money to go around, people will be limited in how many books they can buy a year. It's up to you, with this creative brief in hand, to get that across. After you accomplish that, then it will be up to your writing to handle the rest.

EXERCISE FOURTEEN

1. What is the Background Reasoning for your brand to exist?
2. What is your Brand Objective?

3. What are your Brand Goals?
4. Who are your Target Demographics?
5. Primary
6. Secondary
7. What is your Brand's Tone?
8. What is some of your Brand Messaging?
9. What Visuals best represent your brand?
10. How can you measure the performance of your Brand Goals?
11. What are your Production Parameters?
12. Schedule & Timing
13. Budget
14. Deliverables

WORKSPACE

BRAND POSITIONING STATEMENT

From your creative brief, you can form the construct of your brand. This will be found in two deliverables: a brand positioning statement and a brand concept. These are the two elements that will lead into your pre-production phase. Your concept can lead to actual production leading up to a book release, or the start of your brand. The self-publisher can determine exactly how and when everything comes together. An author tied to a publisher does not have that luxury. If you're just getting started, and haven't even started submitting your book for consideration, then the brand launch can be raising awareness for your brand and your future book.

The first is a brand positioning statement. This is an even briefer statement than your brief. It will be only four points to create a singular positioning statement. This is the place you belong within the market.

A brand positioning statement consists of four basic elements that go into your statement, the first of which is your target audience. You've defined your demographic and this isn't far from the same tree. It'll include the summary of who you're aiming to reach, their age, and what the demographic is looking for in your brand. The second element is a category frame of reference. That's fancy lingo for the product you're offering. The third element is the emotional benefit, promise, or rationale. Fourth, and final, is the reason(s) someone should believe you. There should only be a handful of them—don't go too nuts with the reasons to believe. This is because as you formulate your production, you'll find simple and persistent communication is beneficial.

The end result is a breakdown that you can easily understand, but the challenge isn't about whether you understand, but whether your audience understands. Break it down like this: For a (Target Audience), you are the (Category Frame of Reference) that (Rationale). This is because (Reasons).

An easy example would be: *For Middle Grade Readers, 9-12, wanting a grander, vicarious journey from their summer vacations, John Smith writes the escapist fantasy book series that celebrates the friends and family you find in the most important years of your early life. That's because there are relatable characters that form unlikely bonds, increasing stakes with fantastical creatures, a spin on the world readers think they understand, and an intricate narrative that spans multiple installments.*

Don't overthink it or feel completely bound to the formula. However, once you start pushing a page on this thing, you need to dial it back. This is the brand positioning statement. It allows you to find the avenue upon which your marketing will be built. You need to clearly articulate it and do so in a deliberate, meaningful way. If you haven't been able to fill in your Creative Brief or Brand Positioning Statement without mentally meandering, you either haven't done enough research or you haven't found the basic idea yet. Keep trying to revise what you need, and where you need it. This statement defines where your band lives, and why it has a place in the market above the hundreds of other authors competing in your genre.

EXERCISE FIFTEEN

1. What is your brand positioning statement?

WORKSPACE

NAME

If you are pursuing traditional publication, this really boils down to deciding your author name. It's as simple as that. However, within that, you have to think about what your author name conveys. After all, a publisher may prefer a name that's popular for the target demographic, something that's relatable to the age group. It's just the truth: publishers can sell a name like Emma for younger age groups better now than they ever could Gertrude. An extreme example, but it proves the point.

If you choose to use your birth name, understand that will mean that finding your personal social media accounts and information will be easier. You can separate accounts to have one for your personal endeavors and utilize a different page to engage readers, but know that there will always be challenges and you'll have to decide how the personal and professional worlds collide or separate.

If choosing something other than your given name, the challenge becomes finding a name that isn't used and that doesn't sound inauthentic. If you're writing legal thrillers, your author name should sound like a formidable presence in the courtroom. However, if your writing is science fiction humor about space courtroom drama, Blaze

Hunter might be perfect. The author name is a part of the package being sold. Therefore, your author name should embody the catharsis you're providing readers.

Now, if you're self-publishing, making a publishing company named "Smith Publishing" sounds about as exciting as a Three-Toed Sloth Racing Circuit. Being at reading conventions, and introducing yourself as "Author John Smith, I publish through John Smith Publishing," sounds remarkably self-involved as well as something that wasn't well thought out. Go back to the catharsis. When someone reads any one of your books, what is the overall catharsis? That can inform the publishing name. A Western self-published author could have their publishing company named after their childhood horse that made them fall in love with the open prairie. An author specializing in military action could have a publishing company named after a soldier that the writing is dedicated to, or perhaps an infamous city where a battle took place.

No matter your author name and publishing company name, make sure you can register those business names and get an easy URL for them. The more generic your names, the more difficult it will be to register those names. You are separating yourself from the rest, so even if your amazing publishing house name is taken by a bakery, don't fight it. They beat you to it. Unless you have an insane amount of money to put against organic search results, you'll have to find something that isn't searched for regularly. This is a key component of separating yourself from the rest.

EXERCISE SIXTEEN

1. What is your brand name?
2. Why?

WORKSPACE

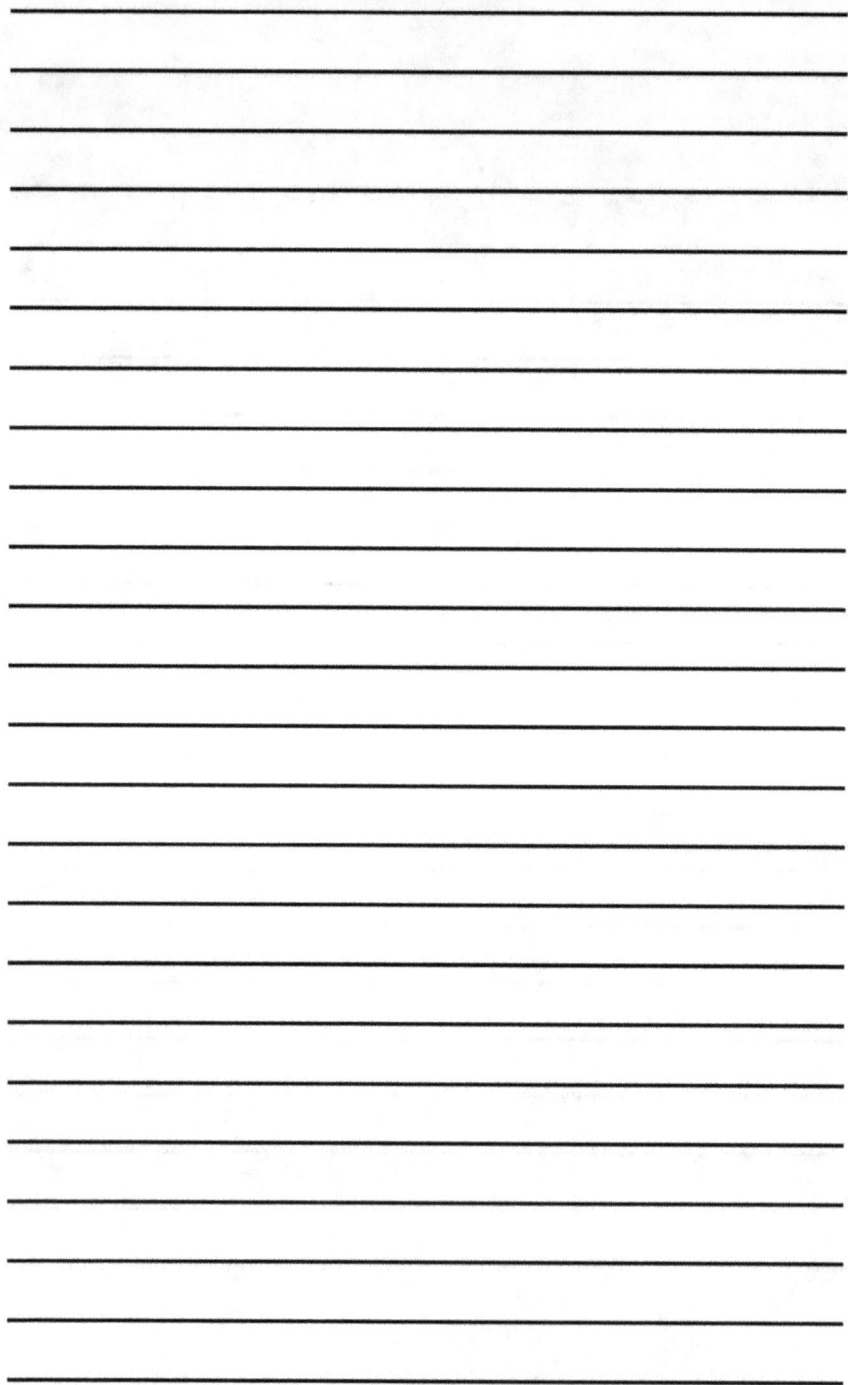

CONCEPT

This positioning statement can then lead to the concept. The most basic iteration of this is to create a bulleted list. Within each listed item is an element of your brand. Those connected tissues will lead into the pre-production process where your marketing is going to be created. First, the easy part: put your brand name up top. If you are an author, you need your name at the top of it all. If you're creating a self-publishing company, put your company name up there.

Now, time to add some connective tissue. These will be the next levels down within the bulleted list. These are the core elements of your brand which will be culled from your strengths and opportunities. You should also make your just completed Brand Positioning Statement handy. The second level of your list needs to include what your brand aims to be. If you want your brand to be known for technological advancement in the reading industry, write that. If you want to elicit a certain emotion, include it. You also need to include the basics. You're flying at 40,000 feet, and now it's time to prepare for landing.

Include elements of what your brand will be known for from a customer interaction standpoint. Possible included elements, such as atmosphere and service, can be included in these categories. They won't define what the atmosphere of the brand is yet; the idea is to recognize that the atmosphere is an important factor. The next levels will allow for separation. To make this simple, the second tier is broken into five, easy-to-fill categories. Adjust if you want, but this will give you an idea of what to do as your concept comes together.

The first thing to look at is Category. If you're a fiction author, write that. If you're specifying that you want to exclusively write video games, put that in. This is a very broad approach. Ideally you're starting with a single category because we're going into another level after this, with possibly two more layers. Remember that if you get too specific, you start pigeonholing your brand. Tons of brands can be built on doing just one thing and doing it better than the rest. So, if you plan on only writing space exploration science fiction, make that your category. Just know the second you write a book in a different setting, your brand concept is back to the drawing board. Plan ahead and think about what you want to write. If you're unsure, Author or Writer is a fantastic start.

The second thing to look at is Experience. The three examples provided are Brand Leader, Technological Leader, and Literary Example. Experience is what your brand will be known as from an experiential standpoint. If you want to lead a revolution in your genre, Brand Leader is a good line item. If you plan on creating interactive elements which include clickable experiences in reading, connected audio experiences, or children's reading apps, describe yourself as a Technological Leader. A Literary Example brand would be someone looking to be revered by critics and an award-winning author.

The third to look at is Delivery. What will people say about the way you deliver your product(s)? Delivery can be an amazing confirmation of a consumer experience. They hope you provide exactly what they want. You have an opportunity to exceed their expectations. That's optimal delivery of your product. Do you self-publish and therefore pride your brand with your level of service? Do you create an atmosphere on your website that hasn't been seen? Do you release products only when they are of the utmost quality? How do you deliver your brand to your consumer?

The fourth element is Emotion. When people talk about your brand, what emotions do they associate with it? It shouldn't necessarily be the emotion they directly associate with your books, but your advertising experience. This, of course, means your brand doesn't have to be completely removed from what you write. In fact, it should be in your broader milieu.

Emotion can be a perception of Comfort. There are books that make you tense, and there are books you go back to in order to feel warm and cozy. You can find an escape in books (and your brand). It can be luxury, a vibrant brand that lives within a vivacious world of high society. It can be Value, in which your marketing provides lower cost experiences that allow for easier access to the product than those only selling hard covers. Don't mistake that for cheapness—it's value. Perhaps your brand displays vintage with pride. Your brand is a throwback to a simpler time. This is an emotional experience that you give consumers with open arms.

The fifth thing to look at is Personality. What is your personality? How can it be conveyed in your marketing? Remember, your brand is entirely based on you. If you have a thrilling personality, send it into your marketing and brand. If you soak up experiences most consider too risky, convey that in your messaging. Channel whatever it is you possess so that readers are called to action to join you in your cause.

You now understand the secondary categories for your brand concept. These five bullets suggested are exactly that: suggestions. If you want more than one emotion, pick more than one. If your brand fits into a category not included, go for it. Never take anyone's word as completely mandatory. This is your creative *guide* for your journey in the business world.

Most of the best brands and advertising thought of something someone else hadn't done yet. Consider this a challenge to do it even better than anyone ever has. Here's an example chart with the secondary tier of your brand concept:

- o BRAND NAME
    - Category: Author, Writer, Blogger
    - Experience: Brand Leader, Technological Innovator, Literary Example
    - Delivery: Service, Atmosphere, Quality
    - Emotion: Comfort, Value, Luxury, Vintage
    - Personality: Thrilling, Lively, Angry
    - Maybe you put down less than five secondary categories in your brand concept, maybe you have more. Either way, you have your concept. Now, how are you going to put this into action?

You want to enter the fantasy YA category. Great, you've chosen your path. Why should anyone choose your book over the hundreds—likely thousands—of other authors who are in that exact same brand category? What are you offering that even has an inkling of an edge over the competition? This isn't asked to make you feel overwhelmed or hindered; it's an answer you have to be able to provide. The truth of the matter is that consumers are going to ask that exact question when deciding about engaging with your brand or not. Your brand concept has nothing to stand on if what you want to be known for has no avenue to answer how you're going to execute your concept. Having said that, this tertiary level is actually how you'll reach your actionable level on a concept.

The first category is easy. You're an author. Now you need to define what, specifically, readers will associate with your being an author. This can include any number of elements (character, sci-fi, epic, comedy, etc). These are the consistent pieces that people will use to describe your author brand.

The same thing applies with the Experience category. If you want to be a Technical Leader, your tertiary level should include the tactics and association people will make. Social media, interaction, innovation, trends... you can seek to embrace social trends that embrace fast thinking. You can be replying to hashtags on social media.

For Delivery, your service level can be professional, responsive, and/or options. Your Emotion categories provide comfort with a sense of community, relaxation, and consistency. Again, these tertiary categories are yours to fulfill. By doing so, you now have your brand concept. It is a concept, and therefore something that needs to transform from an idea into tangible deliverables.

EXERCISE SEVENTEEN

1. What is your brand name? (Copy from exercise sixteen.)
   a. What is your category?
      i. What are the specifics of your category?
   b. What is your brand experience?
      i. What are some avenues to achieve this experience?
   c. How do you deliver the experience of your brand?
      i. What are the methods of delivery?
   d. What is your key brand emotion?
      i. What are some key emotional takeaways?
   e. What is your brand personality?
      i. What are some key personality descriptors?

WORKSPACE

LOGO

This may appear to be a non-issue, especially if you aren't starting a self-publishing company. However, imagine your favorite coffee shop with no logo. While some companies survive with simple text treatment, it is rare. In those instances, the other elements of the company brand are strong enough to offset other absent elements, such as a logo. There may not be a major design element to your author logo—a text treatment of your name could be the simple answer. The font will inform quite a bit in terms of what you're trying to convey.

There are four major categories of fonts; within each category resides sub-categories. The four major types will allow you to understand the core elements of what they convey.

Serif: The most traditional. This font group contains the infamous Times New Roman. This font type is classic, traditional, and reliable. There are few Serif fonts that can be considered outside of acceptable norms. Many actually attempt to recreate the fonts that were used when books were made on traditional press printers, one letter at a time. An author text treatment in a Serif font will show you have a respect for the past, and honor time-old traditions. Some iteration of Serif fonts even have a retro feel, bringing a sense of classical tradition into the modern world.

Sans Serif: A variation of the traditional Serif fonts, the second group has a more geometric approach. With blockier corners and edges, some are considered difficult to read. These are based more on Roman types, and some can help with futuristic, computerized appearances. The geometric approach is perfect for a more calculated author text treatment.

Script: Script font treatments encapsulate written styles. The formal approach—some including calligraphy—derive from traditional handwriting. Many others include old English type with formalized calligraphy at their base. Appearing as if a squire should read them, script has its place for more historical authors. There are casual versions of script font treatments, which have a better base within more casual writing.

Decorative: The fourth and final category is the grab bag of what's left. This category can encapsulate a stylized author to perfection. It can also be a terrible, terrible way to go. It completely depends on the quality of the font, as finding a decorative font will likely mean shopping for one to use. There are many grunge types that would be great for the apocalyptic writer. Some are more psychotic, perfect for the horror writer creating a mental institution series. Again, tread carefully, because for every great decorative font there are 50 terrible ones.

Should your logo need more than just a font treatment, the logo elements have to be considered. Would clean lines to an almost corporate appearing logo seem like you're creating an establishment for others to follow? Would a splatter with the hand of an undead creature rising from the ground encapsulate the horrors you write every day? Iconic imagery can make all the difference. Think of the moment man first walked on the moon. You can see the drop from the last rung of the ladder, the bulky suit bouncing on the surface from the lower gravity. Look at propaganda posters; their style shows you the way to a brighter future through rebellion against the opposing faction. Look up imagery that impacted you and ask why. An image or design to your author logo can help a reader understand what they're going into. A great logo will help consumers not just understand what they'll be reading, but what experience they'll be receiving.

EXERCISE EIGHTEEN

1. What company logos are closest to what you envisioned from your brand?
2. What is the design like?
3. What do the lines look like (sharp, curved, wide)?
4. How do those logos cue the consumer to what the brand does?
5. For your brand logo, what elements will remain throughout your writing? A science fiction writer fixated on space could say "spaceship."
6. What visual cues can you give the consumer with your logo?
7. If your logo could partner with any brand in the world (writing or otherwise), what would it be? Why?
8. What elements of that partner brand can be translated to your brand?
9. When you look at your planned career as a writer, what do you envision as a logo that could carry with that writing for years—if not decades—to come?

WORKSPACE

_____

_____

_____

_____

_____

_____

_____

_____

_____

_____

_____

_____

_____

_____

_____

_____

_____

_____

_____

_____

_____

_____

_____

COLORS

Each season has certain colors associated with it. Winter is depicted by white snow against grey skies. With spring, you think of green leaves; colors popping from flowers as they bloom. Summer allows for long days of yellow sun and blue skies. Fall brings about red leaves and darker sunsets. Your author brand needs color. Different colors evoke different emotions.

Take a look at restaurants. There is a reason the vast majority of restaurants embrace warmer colors, as they're proven to psychologically trigger happier thoughts and have a direct impact on hunger (or the perception of hunger).

The counter-point to the yellows, oranges, and reds of many restaurants is green. With a societal emphasis among certain demographics for healthy, clean eating, green has its place among restaurants. It evokes a sense of environmental consciousness and health. Red logos evoke excitement, those rare treats and indulgences you crave.

Blues and greys are steadfast, providing a quieting sense of balance. They are the brands that are there for you. When smaller businesses and startups come and go, those are the companies that remain strong and keep a consistent experience.

The colors of your logo, brand and website spark emotion. It is an emotion that is indicative of the experiences that lie ahead. Here are some colors and very common companies that use the color for primary use. Read through these colors and learn from them. As you hear about emotion you enjoy and fits your writing, mark them down.

Brand colors should have a primary and highlight color, and that's it. You can get away with a third color if you go with black or white for the third, or a small accent like the green leaf on a logo. However, few logos have gone with multiple color schemes , and when they do, they embrace it. They deliberately design multiple colors to show the diversity of the palette. The diversity of the colors has to be embraced, so if you're thinking of a four-color brand that's just warm colors, rethink it.

Black: The second most common color used in brands, black is crisp with sharp lines. It's classic and that timelessness works. Reminiscent of classic text, black is a sophisticated color and commonly seen with motor vehicles, technology, and sports companies. Black is common among brands showing a sense of authority. Many publishers use black for their color either exclusively or with an accent splash of red. Text treatments in black beckon to printed works and make a lot of sense for authors to use. However, since it is so common, the trick becomes separation in the design.

Blue: Like the ocean, blue is a color that is secure, dependable and responsible. It is also the most commonly used brand color among all other major colors. Brands that use blue include major home

improvement stores, utilities, social media, medical drug manu-
facturers, automobile companies, snacks, television networks,
retailers, financial institutions, and space exploration. Blue
obviously works, as evidenced by the absurd amount of brands
using the color. A lighter blue gives the illusion of a light sky, a
breezy environment. Deeper blues are good for environmental
brands. Brands with a more standard blue are like water: ever-
present and there when needed the most.

Brown: Like purple, brown is one of the least used colors in brands.
It has an earthiness to it that conveys a grounded nature. With
that comes reliance on the brand. Many providers like shipping
companies and clothing brands that use the color, as it shows they
thrive on reliance and security. Brown is often seen in the
branding of food and beverage companies, specifically chocolate
and coffee. Brown, when used with a savory approach, can
instigate desire for comfort. Some sports teams embellish brown
in their logo as well, showing their heartiness.

Orange: Orange is positive color, associated with vibrant sunsets,
colorful fruit and fiery spirit. As a result, you see a lot of
companies with focus on either family or adventurous lifestyles.
You'll also see orange used for children's programming and
family-oriented shoe stores. The adventurous lifestyle choice
comes with companies like photo services, outdoor gear, and
motorcycles. They provide the life you want, albeit in a variety of
delivery methods. There are a few technology-focused areas that
use orange, likely for the friendliness of the color. Those logos
include multiple sound, technological, and home entertainment
brands. Either way, this is what you notice: they're inviting.

Pink: Pink is becoming a bit of a sensitive subject in marketing. This is because as women seek confidence, the traditional feminine association with pink is wavering. Retailers are now disassociating toy sections by gender, removing the distinctive pink and blue from their designs. The common thread that pink is exclusively feminine is still perceived; however, this can be alienating to some women. The traditional perception of pink is that of romance, something suggestive of care-taking. Pink still has its place, of course. There are multiple logos utilizing pink as a sense of empowerment as well (such as women's foundations and newer female clothing companies skewed toward enablement). This is where understanding your market and demographics will be beneficial. There are a few food companies that use pink, typically for sweeter emphasis (such as donut and ice cream shops). Pink sparks happiness over the excitement of indulgence to come.

Purple: Likely not the most obvious choice. There is a history of nobility and royalty in association with purple, as well as an association with wisdom and value. This nobility can be seen with universities and higher-end liquors. Value can be seen with food, shipping companies, beauty and hair products, as well as a few websites that skew toward business service rather than entertainment. There are a few outliers in there including sports teams, cable networks, and several candy companies.

Red: You think of passion, a romantic gesture. You also think of boldness, a strong choice to make a strong statement. Red calls attention to itself. It's used to spark hunger and excitement. Over 17 internationally known food brands—including restaurants, fast-food chains, snack and beverage companies—use red as the primary color for their brand. Are you hungry yet? Red also evokes excitement. You see this excitement in energy drinks and sports clothing companies. There are a few others that are all about excitement, such as camera companies, major retailers, video streaming services, and gaming companies.

Yellow: The sun is warm; it provides sustenance. Therefore, you see yellow being used by mostly two types of companies: comforting foods and reliable providers. Examples include electronics, motor vehicle manufacturers; tire companies, home furnishings, shipping companies and photographic equipment. For a wide variety of industries, their logos are very clean and show a sense of strength and stability. Food is where you feel the warmth of the color. Examples include fast food, sandwich chains, chips and snacks, and breakfast-focused restaurants. They offer stability; their menus and offerings have some key items that keep people coming back.

White: Another common color seen in multiple brand logos. However, white is seen most often in connection with other colors, as most backgrounds are white; white has to be put against something to be visible. There is simplicity and purity in the color white. It is clean. It is vibrant and shines. Some brands even use subtle grays for a controlled, calming treatment. Computer companies embrace white in their logos and advertise with clean gray splashes. Sometimes simplicity is a much louder voice.

The color(s) you choose will help emanate your brand voice. Vibrant colors show a fun, expressive brand. Calm colors display sophistication. Bold colors make for strong statements. You write what you love, you write the books you want to read. The color(s) of your brand should be extensions of what you write, and therefore extensions of yourself. When they see your selected colors, readers will say, "That makes sense. Those colors are perfect."

EXERCISE NINETEEN

1. What color best represents your brand?
2. Do you only need that color?
   a. Why or why not?
3. If needed, what secondary color would help emphasize your first brand color choice?
   a. Is it complimentary or contrary?
   b. What does the nature of the second color say about your brand?
4. Do you need a third color?
   a. Is it black or white?
   b. If not black or white, are you going for a colorful motif? If so, what is your reasoning? (This is rare, so please justify.)
   c. Can your brand just use two colors, then a black or white to outline or emphasize?
      i. If so, which one?
      ii. If not, do you feel a multi-colored logo will work best?
5. How do these colors tie into your logo concept?
6. If they don't, what needs to change?
   a. Should you modify your logo to accommodate the colors you chose?
   b. Should you modify your colors to accommodate the logo concept?

WORKSPACE

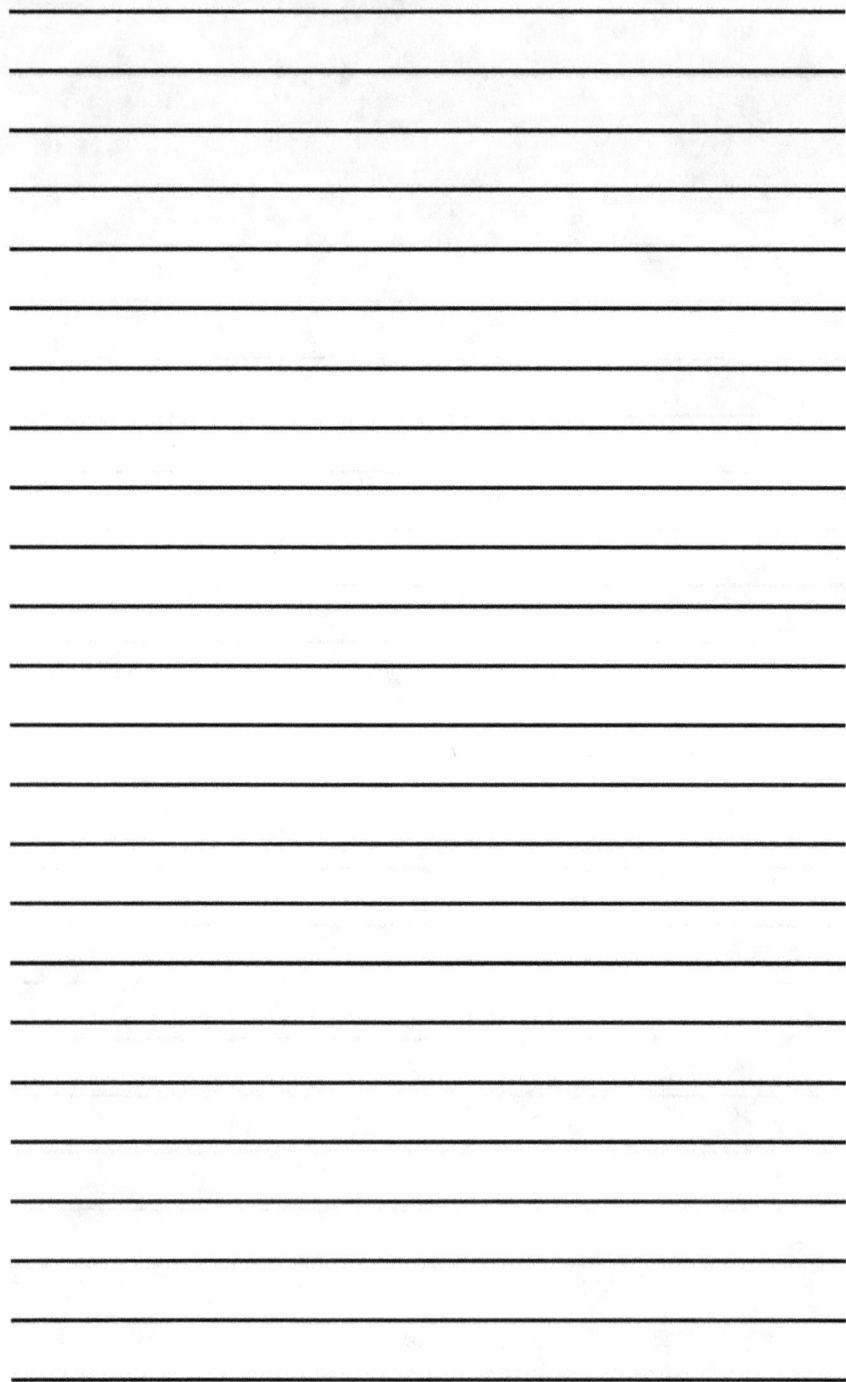

TAG LINE

There are memorable tag lines that become as synonymous and necessary as the brand itself. Many tag lines also include the product. Many resonate so well, practically every company without an original thought created a derivative campaign of those tag lines. They sparked the public interest because they either created iconic imagery, or perfectly encapsulated the brand voice. Within a tag line, other headlines can be put into ads; however, the tag line stays with the brand for a long duration. It is part of the brand essence. It should be something universal enough that as more books come out, it is still understood as to what you provide overall.

The tag line conveys the brand essence clearly. In the case of many sports companies, the tag line discusses the lifestyle of buying the product. When you wear their sporting equipment or clothing, you choose to take action in life, to be striving for a healthy lifestyle. It has been a part of a company brand for years because it still encapsulates the company approach.

Therefore, a tag line is something with a bit more consistency than a campaign in advertising. It is something that can, and should, remain for a long time.

With that, understand what your brand wants readers to know you for. It's not enough to say "John Doe, Author of Mysteries." That would be you and a few thousand others. This is where specificity of your brand concept comes into play. Tell a story and keep it simple. Make that story unique. The essence of good writing still applies. "Jonathon Doemus—Mysteries of Myth" will stick with people. You're clear about what you offer. Yes, that will turn away people who don't read mysteries, but you're not targeting them anyway. Consider this a single sentence story about you, the author.

If none of those seem to work, focus on another round of drafting tag lines. Try to see if focusing on what you write only, rather than your authorship, stands out. Ask those who've read your work what they think of when they think of you, the author, as well as how they feel when they read your manuscripts. Eventually, something will click. When you explore that spark and revise, eventually you'll land on a tag line you can stick with for a long time.

EXERCISE TWENTY

1. Write 10 tag lines.
2. Which 3 were your favorites?
   a. Why? What is it about them that you liked?
3. What are your 3 least favorites?
   a. Why? What is it about them that didn't resonate?
4. Write 10 more tag lines. If you're stuck, explore alternatives for your 3 favorites.
5. Which 3 were your favorites from the second batch?
   a. Why?
6. Do they beat your first batch of 10?
   a. What made them better?
7. Are there elements, keywords or emotions missing that fit your color or logo ideas, which can then be implemented?
   a. Which ones?

8. Write 10 more. Again, explore variations of your 6 favorites if you're stuck.

   a. Which 3 are now your favorites?

9. You now have 9 potential tag lines. Is there one that made you jump in cathartic excitement?

   a. If yes, which one?

      i. Does it need refining? If so, write 10 variations of this favorite tag line. If none are better, choose the original favorite.

   b. If no, write 10 more tag lines, repeat as necessary.

WORKSPACE

VOICE

T he tag line should be the first indicator as to brand voice. All other advertising materials should emphasize this voice. Brand voice is the way your advertising sounds to consumers; the language of your marketing. This should be an extension of your existing persona. The world needs diversity in writing to accommodate different tastes. Brand voice should be an extension of the writing you love to create.

The voice will carry into longer copy beyond tag lines and simple headlines. It carries into your website body copy. Your social media should embrace your brand voice. Use your natural voice. Social media users will discover you, and engage you when they find what they like.

Engagement is key; brand voice should invite readers in. With a friendly voice, simple language, and purposeful messaging, your brand will create a community. The voice of that community will consequently help you find the right audience. This is why voice is so important. Angry posts on social media and a bitter tone will summon others who respond to that tone. The reverse influence can occur as well. A positive tone with invitational action verbs can create a community of support. Trolls may try to bring the community down, but with a strong brand voice comes a unified tribe, unwilling to embrace hatred.

Creating a series of rules and key words for your brand voice is essential. That way, with each post, display advertisement and giveaway, there is consistency. Your tag line should be included wherever appropriate. You can try a series of keywords for a few months; see if the blog posts get more engagement than the last few. See if a hashtag sticks with more follows and shares than others. Brand voice can shift as you move along; it cannot remain static. At the same time, you are selling books. There are ways to say that, but there will be some repetition. This is where the author and the copywriter will have to be separated. Writing narrative works is a different experience than advertising. This is because with a novel, you have pages upon pages to immerse the reader in your world. In advertising, you have a headline and a call-to-action. Therefore, brand voice should be the simplest means of communicating your author voice.

Tone will help evoke that. If your writing is subversive, brand voice should exemplify that tone. If your advertising seems calm and polite, not testing the system, then the subversive nature of your writing won't come through and your books will be lost in the shuffle. There is no reason for your creative writing not to reflect the same passion as in your marketing.

EXERCISE TWENTY-ONE

1. Write a paragraph describing your brand. Sell someone on your life's work.
    a. Does it match the tag line, colors, and logo concepts you've created? If not, refine the voice to match.

2. Write headlines for each book you've written or plan to write.

    a. Do they fit the tone of your brand paragraph, tag line, colors, and logo concepts? If not, what needs to change? This doesn't have to be an exact match, but readers should say, "It makes sense that THAT author wrote that book."

WORKSPACE

_____

_____

_____

_____

_____

_____

_____

_____

_____

_____

_____

_____

_____

_____

_____

_____

_____

_____

_____

_____

_____

_____

_____

_____

BRAND STRATEGY

Y ou're getting married. Congratulations. Whether this is true or not, play along for a minute. The ceremony is coming up in a few months, so it's time to find a venue. Most venues can book up to a year out, sometimes longer. Time to adapt. All the good venues are booked, but you can't move the date. You have to have a strategy and time, depending on what your approach will be. That's where brand strategy comes into play.

All too often, writers believe that if the writing is good then the rest will fall into place. To an extent, that's true. However, without a good marketing strategy, the initial pitch of your book won't appeal to either an agent or reader. A great book that cannot sell is a hard pitch to send a publisher's way.

There are several elements you have to put into place for your brand strategy. They will be formulated from the initial research phase and the S.W.O.T. and P.E.S.T. analysis you've completed. These research elements will transform into logical marketing steps. These steps are needed to create loyalists—those who are wholeheartedly dedicated to your writing. The question has to be answered as to who your loyalists will be. This depends on where you are in your career and how you want to focus your brand at the time.

It all boils down to the core element of a brand: your primary goal. If you're a writer, it's likely that your primary goal is the same as the writer sitting beside you in critique groups: to sell your books. If you're an established author, you have a primary goal to sell your books, they're just aimed at a different demographic. The aspiring ones are looking for publishers and editors to buy the work. Once achieved, your demographic changes to a reading audience.

It sounds simple, but can be easily forgotten. Stray just a little, and before you know it you're meandering about in social media, your query letter is inconsistent with the synopsis and submissions process, blog posts are erratic and inconsistent, etc. You have to focus in on your primary goal with every ounce of your effort. Secondary goals can tie in to your temporary efforts or campaigns. That's where you can modify your strategy to the goal you have to accomplish at a specific juncture. However, *everything* has to feed in to the primary goal.

This primary goal is accomplished with five steps to increase your brand's presence, create conversations, and establish loyalists who will be dedicated to you, your books, and your brand. It is a natural process, much like dating. There will be awkward times when you find out if you want to keep seeing each other. Then you'll start finding out more about one another. Then it's time to see if it can go from dating to a relationship. It's exciting, the chemistry is undeniable; however, long-term relationships are no easy feat. The next steps of your brand strategy are to head into the scary portion of a relationship in which there is dedication. Of course, then come the real leaps to engagement and marriage. It may seem farfetched, but like I said, the venue has to be booked early. So, get ready for some commitment as your brand strategy comes together.

EXERCISE TWENTY-TWO

1. How long do you realistically have to put a brand strategy together?
2. What are the best parts of your writing? (Copy from exercise five.)
3. How can those play into strategic brand decisions?

WORKSPACE

RECOGNITION

T he first of the five steps to creating a brand strategy is recognition. In order for a reader to find your book, they have to know it exists. Recognition takes an inordinate amount of effort. One of the oldest adages in marketing is the "Rule of Seven," which means that someone has to be exposed to your specific marketing seven times before they decide to act. Therefore, the first hurdle is just to get recognition. If the answer was quantity, in theory just placing advertisements everywhere would be the solution. However, you have to remember the subject. It's not only about the amount of times they see the advertising, it's recognition. Consumers have to recognize a distinguished, singular form of messaging.

With this recognition, there will be a series of elements to identify. First of all, you have to gain the emotional core of your advertising. What are key factors that will help users get behind your book and your brand? This will help decide elements that you can use for creating your website, promotional tools, and a voice behind the messaging.

Throw the notion of a marketing budget out the window. Imagine that you have infinite amounts of money at your disposal. Who would your spokesperson be? Who would be the celebrity that would endorse your book, telling the world about what you've written and why it's important. I know it seems weird to think of something that will likely never happen, but stick with me here—there's a reason for this approach.

Emotional messaging. There's a reason certain people are cast to embrace a brand. They're able to encapsulate an emotional resonance. When your book is a mystery involving murder, a high-pitched, awkward teenager won't exactly scream, "Buy this frightening narrative." An epic science fiction with a female protagonist could be amazingly represented by an actress who was on a prestigious sci-fi show with martial arts training. You wouldn't choose a straight-laced fatherly figure. That's why you choose your dream spokesperson. Whether they work on promotional materials doesn't matter; this exercise helps you understand how you have to begin gathering your messaging.

Many authors write to music. Can it find a place within your brand? Either through a track for a book trailer, or ambient music on an audio book, sound can set the mood or emphasize catharsis. Think of the perfect song you would use if money were no issue. You know your book; you know the experience you want to bring to your authorship. Select the song you want as your ideal book trailer. Sure, publishers will help you create a book trailer. What better tool can you give them to understanding the approach than a source track to draw inspiration from? If you know what you're conveying, you can help translate that into tangible deliverables.

Several websites offer composed music for you to purchase at a fraction of what it would cost for a movie score. Careful searches for a "sounds like this artist" in your browser can narrow the tracks you have to sift through. Then, if you're self-publishing, you can use that track to edit, or have someone edit, your book trailer. A firm hit against the keys of a piano can disrupt an ambient crackle; that's when your villain reveals himself in the book trailer. The quirky walk-and-talk transforms into a softer composition, signaling the start of your less comedic scenes. The moment they feel ready for a final, climactic moment is when the music quiets down and an offer to purchase the book comes along.

The odds of you getting a major studio track for your trailer are slim. However, never look at the unattainable and think of it as such. That music can have a variety of functions including inspiration for a video editor, or recommendation to a publishing house's marketing team, or even finding a royalty free music track to edit the book trailer yourself, if your budget is minimal.

Other elements to your marketing can be sensory. What does it smell like? If the pages of your book could be infused with an essential oil, what would that smell be? Is it a sanitary alcohol that tries to hide the seedy underbelly? As readers flip the page, think of what smell would escape.

What about taste? Simultaneously, what would the pages feel like? Write down the four-course meal your writing tastes like. It could be a delicately prepared cuisine, or it could just as easily serve up a hearty feast of meals only available to the most savage hunters.

As the senses of your brand become evident, they translate to the marketing approach. Your layouts, fonts, social media imagery, the works… these senses should be infused within your brand. Create a social media imagery board. Give your brand a look. What images appear to fit with your brand? What environments best suit it? This way, as readers and social media followers look at your brand and your marketing, they recognize it. Identifying elements encourage recognition. This is key, so that as you work toward a conversion (customer buying your book, or social media user following you, etc.) the first step is recognition. By doing so, this will transition to the next phase of customer interaction: awareness.

EXERCISE TWENTY-THREE

1. If money were no object, who would your spokesperson be?
   a. Why are they the perfect fit for your brand?
   b. How would their representation help people to recognize your brand and what it offers?
2. If your books came to life, what would they look like? What would the reader see?
3. Your words are harnessed and channeled through a sound system. What sounds would you hear?
4. Imagine that, as your readers turned the pages of your books, the pages didn't feel like paper, but like the world they're immersing themselves in. What do those pages feel like?
5. Every page of your novel has a smell. What does the reader smell?
6. If you had a meal to serve that fit the tone of your novel, what would that meal be?
7. What do people recognize about you, as a person physically?
8. What emotions make you instantly recognizable?
9. How will people recognize your work?
10. What marketing phrasing, imagery or approach will allow people to distinctively recognize as your brand?

WORKSPACE

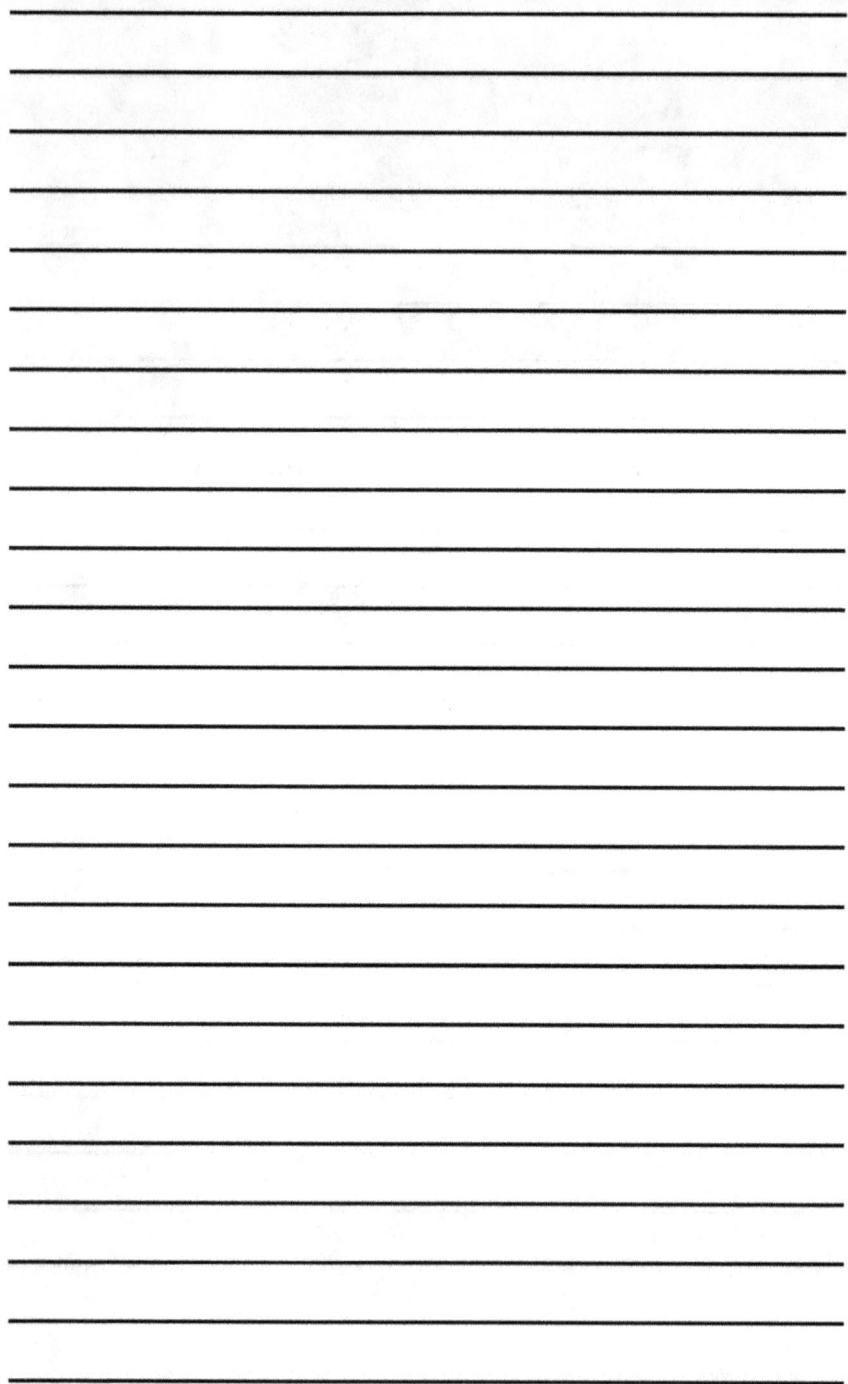

AWARENESS

Recognition and awareness sound like the same thing. However, there is a key difference in the five steps to creating loyal readers and regular consumers of your product. Recognition crafts a series of identifying elements readers can see. Awareness is the next process and deals more with your content. Awareness provides the chance for the consumer to know how they're interacting with your brand. Recognition is to form a singular identity; awareness makes your fans knowledgeable about what you provide.

The elements you create in recognition will now find a voice through your brand. This can be the easier portion in that the development of awareness comes from your copywriting. This writing will take over your website, your social media and your marketing. All copy has to fill a want or need. The consumer will have to want to buy your book. Therefore, your brand has to convey how that want is fulfilled. In order to do that, they have to be aware of what you are offering. Again, many of these notions sound so simplistic. At the same time, think of how many times you've seen an ad or a brand website and not understood what you were supposed to do with that ad or brand. You see an emotionally intriguing piece that pulls at your heartstrings, but have no idea what you're supposed to buy.

This ties back to the primary goal of your brand: sell your books. If you chose something else for your primary goal, congratulations on the unusual approach and I hope it works. Remember, this isn't your primary writing goal, it's your primary marketing goal. Your writing can have a comedic presence throughout. That's great because it means your author voice has been honed and discovered, but it's unlikely you picked up this book because you want to raise the amount of social media followers to download your free book. Your primary writing goal can be to create literary brilliance, but you also have to eat. This isn't the exquisite portion of the writing process. This is the necessary work to fuel your desire to write for a living.

Such a statement doesn't mean you have to just plug some copy into a layout and call it good. Far from it, the strategic decisions and research from previous chapters will help inform your approach to creating your marketing. How can your strengths be used to raise awareness on your website? How can technological environments make an unsuspecting consumer discover your ad, and be holistically aware of the product you're offering? Strong awareness allows for you to overcome a weakness and help consumers know what emotional need your brand offers. Whether it is religious mysteries, legal thrillers or romantic drama, those fill a definitive emotional want that the reader is seeking. It's up to you, the writer of the brand marketing, to help them understand the emotional want your book fulfills.

Marketing awareness is also very brief. You have a finite amount of time to sell your product. Therefore, as much as you love your prose and believe that there are multiple facets of your narrative that must tie in together perfectly, odds are whatever you write from the marketing standpoint is too long. Therefore, it's best to use the "less is more" approach with the following exercise. Write the briefest copy you can imagine. Now, see if you can cut that in half. Repeat as necessary until you have the most concise version imaginable. If it's adequate for an elevator pitch—it's about 30 seconds read aloud— it's too long, unless you're making a radio spot. What's in the copy? Is it all devoted to the story? That's great for your creative writing, but worthless for your marketing.

Two key elements are headlines and a CTA (Call-To-Action). The headline is your hook, the intriguing line that grabs readers' attention. That is where you should get specific about your brand and your books. If you go for generic statements then it will fall into the mud and disappear among all the other books in your genre. A headline like "The New Science Fiction from Author John Smith" means absolutely nothing unless the name is well-known. However, if the headline involves the specifics of the book and the niche it carves in the market, then it suddenly becomes intriguing. *"The Darwin* entered a black hole. No one expected them to return." Suddenly you have an idea of what the book is about, and the reader will want to know more. The CTA is the communication to the reader to engage the ad. They are simple and fast. If your book is up for pre-order, it can be as simple as "Pre-Order Here." Clicking that CTA would then take them to a page where the user can easily get their copy ordered. Your brand has to invite the reader, or consumer, to engage your brand in a conversion.

Now, this is another category that will depend on your status. If your measure of success is with an agent requesting a manuscript, that's a different CTA than a self-published book hitting the market. Those temporary goals are more campaign-focused, rather than brand. However, notice that they are doing one very easy-to-understand action: fulfilling the primary goal. If you are seeking an agent then your marketing approach is to sell to them first. Self-publishers directly connect to the consumer. That's the key to good marketing: it should hit an emotional want or need, and make the consumer (whether that consumer is an agent, editor, or reader) aware of how they can fulfill that need with your product. Finally, it is fulfilled with what they need to do to buy your book.

The brand and marketing should make the consumer aware that they can buy the book on which platforms. If they engage your marketing then it should go directly to the shop they are seeking, whether that be your publisher directly or an eBook seller. Again, what those actions lead to depend on the circumstances of your brand and whether your primary goal is selling your book in the marketplace or directly to the consumer. Regardless, good awareness in a brand is easy to identify. The emotional need is fulfilled; they know what they're getting and how they are going to get it. If you've done that, they recognize your brand, they are aware of what is offered, and then it's on to the third phase of creating loyal readers: differentiation.

EXERCISE TWENTY-FOUR

1. Who will be the consumer in your marketing?
2. Who is the secondary consumer? (e.g. Gathering readers in your genre via social media and a blog while you sell your book.)
3. Who are you trying to get to buy your book specifically?
4. What are they responding to well on social media?
5. What books are they sharing in posts or adding to their shelves on social media?

6. How can you write messaging that speaks to these consumers directly?

7. What are some keywords you've seen used in books within your genre's advertising?

8. What elements of novels and authors are readers in your genre copying directly?

9. If they aren't copying directly, how are they interpreting what is being advertised versus what is being shared and engaged by readers?

10. Write an "elevator pitch" for your brand (no more than 30 seconds long read aloud).

11. What are five headlines that will capture your readers? (Use the keywords and shares you've found above for guidance. These should also be short. Multiple ad platforms don't allow more than 25 characters, spaces included.)

12. What is your call-to-action? (Maximum of 4 words, preferably less. Should be able to tie into headlines.)

WORKSPACE

DIFFERENTIATION

Congratulations, your social media followers and potential readers have recognized your brand and know what you're offering. Now comes another really difficult question: why should they buy your book over the other countless narratives offered? Seriously, with self-publishing and more platforms to deliver your work, books are more accessible than ever. Apps that sync to your virtual library allow for eBook and audio book rentals. Tablets and smartphone screens provide the chance for interactive experiences. What has your brand brought to the table that thousands of other authors aren't already offering?

This is where differentiation becomes key. Your brand is built on writing legal thrillers, so what? There are so many people writing that genre, and there are authors who are more well-established than you. What possible reason could a reader have to pick up your book rather than stick with the writers they know and love? While you likely think that your book is amazing and very different from any other legal thriller, consumers don't know that. They can recognize and be aware of what you're offering, but without knowing what separates you from the rest, they'll likely move on.

Sales tactics will often draw comparisons. While this can help authors identify similar writers that they may enjoy, differentiation will prove why your book has something new to offer. This is the section that needs to look at the threats and opportunities identified. Don't just glance at the research you completed, dissect it.

Somewhere in that research is the key, dwelling in the darkness of your research. By knowing your threats in the market, you'll know what to avoid. If there are marketing approaches that successful authors are using in your genre, you don't want to copy too closely, as your approach will appear derivative without differentiation. The threats posed to the marketplace will inform what you should and shouldn't execute in your brand and marketing approaches. Threats in the market can be addressed, but be sure not to attack an author who could be a useful ally. The smart approach to a threat is to know how you can strategically outmaneuver them. By carving a niche for yourself, the competition can't touch you and they'll be working with everything that they have to catch up to you.

This is where you have to find the opportunity within your research for your brand. Think of a product or service, the industry doesn't matter. What matters is that when you discovered the product or service, it was unique and took care of something you didn't know you needed taken care of. As a result, you wanted that product or service. It could be a unique method of streaming digital content, a social media platform, or something for the kitchen. Differentiation creates a space in the market that hasn't been discovered yet.

By knowing your opportunities and threats within your industry, your market, genre and brand, you'll understand how you can create a marketing brand that will see your books reviewed, get you requests for interviews, and most importantly, indicate products that will split from the endless amount of books hitting the market.

This is the third step of five on the road to creating dedicated readers who repeatedly return. Now that you've differentiated yourself from other authors, it's time for followers and readers to attach to your brand. There is one pivotal step remaining in your brand strategy; it is the final hurdle that culminates in everything you've done from intelligent writing to strategic marketing. Crossing this threshold begins with keeping readers by your side.

EXERCISE TWENTY-FIVE

1. Within the genre you write, what specific niche are you fulfilling?
2. Why is that different from what is already available in the market?
3. Why are you writing this specific genre?
4. Why should that matter to the reader? What makes you the one to write this book?
5. How can the above four questions be channeled for a unique hook to your brand?
6. Based on the competition you researched previously, what is most commonly being done?
7. How can your marketing create a variation and spin to make your own?
8. What elements of your brand are different than others?

WORKSPACE

_____

_____

_____

_____

_____

_____

_____

_____

_____

_____

_____

_____

_____

_____

_____

_____

_____

_____

_____

_____

_____

_____

_____

_____

ATTACHMENT

Singular transactions aren't enough. In order to have a fulfilling career, you need customers to return. It is proven that it is far easier to retain existing clients than to establish new ones. The effort is substantial. As a result, it's essential you find readers who will attach to your brand. This way, they will recommend your older books as your newer installments come out. Word of mouth is pivotal to any author platform. When someone loves what you offer, they'll recommend you. Think of a series you picked up strictly because someone told you that you should. Odds are you have more than just one series you can name.

The last two steps of Brand Strategy are going to boil down to good writing. Plain and simple, for attachment and insistence to occur in brand strategy, you need a good product. Nothing will help more with attachment and insistence quite like a group of amazing books. However, don't think marketing can't play a pivotal part. If someone won a signed copy your hardback thanks to smart marketing giveaways, don't you think they'll be prone to sharing that experience? Won't they want to tell people about how cool it was to feel the exclusivity of winning something? If your website is easy to understand and has quick links that readers can use to share, won't that make the process of spreading that word of mouth?

This is where your technological and social research come into play. By knowing your strengths as well, you can utilize technology and social spaces to encourage a sense of attachment within your brand. Your strengths can be played up by using technology you can embrace. By doing so, you can create a social movement; one where someone can easily find out about your brand and share it. Social media followers can get shareable, downloadable items such as wallpapers for their computers and smartphones. Within those free, sharable items is a URL to your website. That website has all the links to buy your books and follow you on social media; the web of attachment creates stickiness in which readers attach to your brand.

EXERCISE TWENTY-SIX

1. What can your marketing efforts do to make readers loyal to your brand, not just a single book?
2. How will social media play into those efforts?
3. What technology will make the selling of your books easy and accessible?
4. What promotions can provide opportunities for new people to engage and attach to your brand (giveaways, newsletters, etc.)?
5. How will your marketing build loyalty among readers?

WORKSPACE

INSISTENCE

T hink of a product you will not divert from no matter what. If all that's available are generic substitute products, you will wait. If it's a service like a masseuse or hair stylist and you've attached to a certain individual, you will reschedule an appointment if they're not available. Perhaps there's an author that you've read, and you've tried books that have been compared to the author, but they just don't measure up. These are the authors you insist upon reading every time; you pre-order the hardback. You wait at the bookstore for the chance to get them to sign your book. This is the fifth part of your brand strategy: insistence.

Acquiring loyalists is the final step. There is continued work to be done after securing a loyalist, but from a brand strategy stand-point, this is your closure. This is where you take the research and understand what it will take to make someone a permanent loyalist. Now that you've separated yourself from the market, you've gained the attention of your readers. You've gained social media followers. The step to take is utilizing all elements of the S.W.O.T. and P.E.S.T. analyses to culminate your work. This research will inform the final elements of your brand strategy.

Insistence comes from relevancy. Make your brand relevant to the reader. Marketing is inherently a selfish act—you're telling someone to buy a product you created so that you can benefit. However, you are also writing so that others may share in an experience. You've spent hours upon hours to craft something, and this experience is there for them. Your writing should have emotional relevancy that resonates with your readers. They connect with your writing; they connect with your marketing strategy. Therefore, they connect to your brand.

People seek different books for different elements of relevancy. The consumer may seek information for further intelligence. Perhaps the consumer just lost their mother, and your book explores how life moves forward without the protagonist's mother. There's a reason many writers with storied careers have a trajectory in terms of how their narratives form; they parallel the relevancy of their own lives.

When a writer is young, it's likely the subject matter will be more relevant to that period of existence. As they age, the narratives change with them. They're able to follow a path of relevance as their lives continue forward. The author's works allow for consumers to have a long, fruitful series of experiences that are relevant, and therefore insistence emerges from that relevance.

Brand strategy insistence comes from experience. Your brand is going to deliver a unique experience for the reader. That experience is what they insist upon. Your marketing strategy for the brand has to invite that experience. As you think of authors with incredible followings, you'll likely notice that they have an experience attached to their writing and their brand. It may be comforting, a warm notion of a better life awaiting them beyond a darkness, or it may deliver an experience of gripping unease.

The best authors have a brand that delivers an experience consistently. They may have formed it as a strategic decision, or it may be that the brand experience emerged from their narratives organically. The experience should be a reflection of you. As consumers come to know that experience, they'll become insistent on that experience.

Insistence emerges from catharsis. When you close the back jacket of a book, emotion overwhelms the reader. It can be a sense of horror at the world you just lived in for 400 pages, or a sense of warmth as you move to a greater future. A well-constructed narrative has emotional catharsis, and so should your brand. When a consumer is given a catharsis for purchasing, the brand has exceeded the delivery of the product and marketing. Something was promised, and consumers feel catharsis for receiving what was promised. Catharsis is the emotional closure at the end of a story. A proper catharsis is the pinnacle of the brand experience.

Again, the best way to secure long-term fans is good writing. Marketing and an established brand can get the books into their hands, but good books is what will have consumers return. Market where you can, when you can. Write first. All of these marketing brand strategies can be implemented regardless of the product. However, the marketing has to be backed up by the product itself. Think of a book, movie, or album you couldn't wait to experience, only to be disappointed. The last thing you want is for your marketing to outshine your final product.

Now think of the opposite effect: the opening sequence of a movie was as enthralling as you expected. There are twists you didn't see coming, but remained relevant to the story and enhanced the experience. This is why certain directors are prestigious: the brand of their entertainment has promised a certain experience, and they have delivered. It may not happen every time, but they execute with incredible efficiency toward a catharsis you've come to expect. That's what intelligent brand strategy does: embrace the catharsis you have to offer. When your product delivers on that promise, consumers will insist on your brand and your product.

EXERCISE TWENTY-SEVEN

1. What experience will you provide to readers, that no other author is offering, that will make readers insist upon engaging your brand?
2. How can you provide a sense of exclusivity to your readers, to make following your brand unlike any other?
3. What efforts will you make to retain followers of your brand?
4. What emotional catharsis do you offer readers?
5. How is that different from other authors in your genre?

WORKSPACE

BRAND PRODUCTION

The talking is over. It's time to produce your brand. This production period will help you understand every facet needed to complete your brand. Expect curveballs and unexpected challenges. The first thing you need to do is understand your production budget. Up to this point, many of the steps have been research, concepts and other free elements. Production costs money. As a result, depending on your career status and what money you have, there will be different focuses to take on.

The first step is deciding what you will produce. There's an adage in advertising: things can be done either fast, cheaply, or well. You can combine two of those, but you can never expect all three. If you want an entire brand done quickly, and with incredible quality, expect to shell out money to freelancers to help with the work. If you want to execute your brand well, but can't spend much, expect to sacrifice timing.

You'll have to decide priorities in terms of what to produce. Create three tiers of production: mandatories, preferences, and optional. Mandatories are the elements required for your brand success. Without them, your brand is set up to fail. Preferences are items that will strongly support the brand, but can be sacrificed if you're running low on time or money. Optional items are exactly that. If resources have been depleted, the brand will not be harmed by their omission.

Decide what you can spend as this will help you decide which approach to take. Outside resources can be freelancers, or complete production companies that handle it all. The benefit of doing this yourself is that the labor is free. The downside is that some of the elements of production may prove difficult for you. You may not have the skill sets to execute production efficiently. Another downside to production being handled by you is that you'll take time away from doing what you have to do primarily: write. However, with efficient execution and allowing yourself time to produce, as well as write, it can be done.

Freelancers can be of great help, so long as they are strong freelancers. The best of them rely on word-of-mouth recommendations. Their business and success lives or dies by client perception of execution. Many freelancers have honed a specialty, such as book formatting or proofreading, others have spent their lives learning website coding or art direction. Their knowledge of a specialty field means they can execute a specific task efficiently, and likely with better accuracy than you could yourself. Understand and decide what you can execute effectively yourself. The rest will need outside support.

Vetting outside vendors can be a risky endeavor. Some will provide low cost alternatives to standard pricing. Don't be fooled. If the price seems too good to be true, it likely is. There are some editors or proofreaders that are just getting started. They may charge less, but shouldn't be asking less than fair wage. The truth is to get quality work you have to pay for it. Finding reliable designers, editors and web developers can all be done with the same basic approach. First, speak to those you know; see if they have reliable resources. Word of mouth is an incredible way to find trustworthy people who rely on such recommendations to build their careers. Additionally, freelance websites can help vet vendors. Their reviews, if personalized, can give you guidance on their previous freelance work.

EXERCISE TWENTY-EIGHT

1. What is your total production budget?
2. Are there any determined deadlines or specific timing you have to adhere to?
3. What elements are mandatory to enter production?
4. What elements are preferential?
5. What elements are optional?
6. How much will it cost to get your brand production elements made (logo design, photography, etc.)?

WORKSPACE

BOOKS

Welcome to the first mandatory. Without product to back up your brand, all advertising efforts are white noise. Costs on books will vary greatly depending on your career approach. Traditional publishing comes at a greater cost of time while others complete work. With that come fewer monetary expenses on your part. That statement is under the assumption that the book contract is a decent one. (Side note: you shouldn't have to pay an agent or publisher to read or publish your work.) Self-publishing will include higher costs and take up your time, reducing your ability to write while you focus on the production process.

Regardless of approach, several things need to occur once you finish your book: editing (both content and copy), beta reading, proof-reading, formatting, cover design, cover copy, ISBN code assignment, copyright notice, and illustrations within the book (optional). Ideally you should have already run your book through a critique group. This book is about marketing and brand creation, so these aforementioned steps are to be covered another time. However, after your book has reached a sellable point, regardless of traditional or independent publishing, it can enter the first of many steps to a finished product.

After reaching this point, if you're going the traditional route, it's time to submit. When submitting, some agents and publishers may ask only for a query letter and synopsis. Others may ask for pages. As a result, it would be advantageous of you to create a variety of formats for quick grabbing as you submit. The most common requests are for the first 5, 10, and 15 pages. Some go up to 25, 50, even 100. You can either grab the pages from a master file each time, or create separate documents with each.

You also have to ensure your manuscript is formatted for submission. The steps are quite simple. Now, if you're sending to an agent or publisher, double-check their submission guidelines. There is a decent chance that what is below could be different than what you're submitting. However, using these essential steps will have you ready for the vast majority of agents and publishers. Any variations to the list below should be easily adjusted.

- o Start with a title page.
  - Contact information should be aligned to the left. Single spaced. Should include your actual name (not author name), phone number, e-mail address, and an easy website URL won't hurt if you have it.
  - Word count should be on the right side of the page, at the top as well.
  - Title and author goes halfway down the page. The title should be in all capitals, centered, and double-spaced. Below the title is your author credit.
  - Agent contact name and information goes below the title (if applicable).
  - The title page should not include a header or page count.

- o Every page after the title page should have a header. The header needs your last name, the title of your book (or keywords if it's a longer title), and the page number.
  - New chapters start on their own page 1/3 of the way down the page. Center the chapter title. Skip an extra line before your first paragraph.
  - 1" margins on all sides.
  - Font should be 12pt, black, Times New Roman or Courier New.
  - Each paragraph gets a ½" paragraph indentation.
  - Double-space the entire manuscript. Align text to the left without justification. Justification modifies the text to fill the space, creating awkward spaces and cutting off words.
  - Section breaks get a centered # sign in the center of its own line.
  - Use single character spaces after a sentence. Two spaces after sentences originates back to typewriters and is a dated practice.

Step two will be beta readers. Beta readers are a group of people selected to provide any final feedback on your edited manuscript. The readers should represent two categories: those who are familiar and unfamiliar with your genre. It is vital to hear from horror writers/readers if that is the genre of your book. Consequently, perspective from someone who traditionally doesn't read the genre can be very helpful. Choosing the right 4-6 people to be your beta readers will allow for that final perspective on the manuscript.

If a concern is raised more than once, pay particular attention to that concern/comment.

The feedback can be taken at your discretion.

Step three is content editing. Some have also called this step "structural editing." This edit is focused specifically on the content of the manuscript, checking for consistency in voice, ensuring that events line up linearly, and any other broad notes about the actual content of the book. This makes the manuscript go through drastic changes. As a result, going over apostrophes, sentence structure, and things of that minutia is a moot point. Until the content is ready, it won't matter what the formatting or grammar look like.

If you're going with a traditional publisher, it is likely they will assign you an editor. Self-publishers will have to find an editor. The best route is to talk to the writers you know or contact a local writing organization to see if they have any trusted sources. Word of mouth goes a long way. Costs for editors vary, depending on their experience and qualifications. You should expect to pay $1-2 per formatted page for a decent editor.

Once you have an editor selected, you can discuss costs as well as anticipated times for delivery. Good editors are busy. Expect your manuscript to be put into a queue of projects. This means if an editor gives you a timeframe of 12 weeks, they're not working on your book for a quarter of a year. They likely have multiple projects that were negotiated and on their desk before yours. If you have a release date that requires faster turnaround, that will be a factor as you seek an editor. You'll have to find someone who has fewer projects or faster turnaround times. The content editor will be a determining factor on the quality of your content. Therefore, you need to trust the person who will help shape your manuscript. After submission, the editor will review your manuscript and return comments.

What you do with those comments is up to you. As you read the comments, keep in mind that the content edits are meant to help shape your book into the best product possible. Therefore, trusting the specialist will be to your benefit. If there is an edit that is particularly bothersome for you, reach out to your editor. Clarify why they made that particular edit.

Step four is copy editing. A content editor helps with the bigger picture of your manuscript. A copy editor analyzes sentence composition and grammar. The feedback will be like a thousand little bee stings to your manuscript. Copy editors are the watchdogs. Revisions from the copy editor will be a line-by-line analysis. Once receiving these, you should implement everything they provide. At this point we're talking about the rules of language, not the decisions of a creative personality.

After completing copy editing comes step five: proofreading. Many would argue that copy editing and proofreading are one and the same. However, a proofreader is your final gatekeeper. The copy editor provides feedback, and it is up to you to implement it. The proofreader will catch those final manuscript mistakes you missed. You could read your manuscript 50 times over and you'll still miss a couple of things. The proofreader is the scrutinizing eye, the last revision before sending the manuscript for publication and formatting. After this is done, you can begin final production.

Step six is the cover. Unless you have a background in design, and have proven that competency in a working capacity, don't do it yourself. Hire someone. People do judge a book by its cover. Images sell better than words in advertising. The cover needs to encapsulate the elements of your manuscript and draw the reader to the written words. Think of the cover as the invitation to a party. If the invitation looks lame, the party is likely lame.

Another required item is an ISBN. These are numbers that provide identifying codes to sell your book. Many printing houses provide them. You do need separate ISBN numbers for print and digital. As well, if you are creating any deluxe editions, those will need their own. The key takeaway is that for every singular product, you'll need an ISBN.

The cover copy should also be proofread and edited. You can choose to send that to your editors and proofreaders with your manuscript, or it can be sent as a separate deliverable if you aren't ready to provide it. ISBNs can be purchased separately; many self-publishing book services offer a free ISBN as a part of their service. Figure out the best approach and be sure each version of your book has its own ISBN.

Step seven is formatting. While you format your manuscript a certain way for submission to agents or publishers, formatting a book for publication is completely different. Having someone to format the book for printing and eBook publication will ensure the book reaches vendors accurately. Traditional publication, again, handles this. There are multiple formats required for different devices. As a result, if you're doing it yourself, make sure you have formatted to accommodate all the major platforms.

Step eight is publishing. What goes into publication is another beast. However, depending on your vendor, you will either be able to purchase printed versions of the book in a bulk sale or you can use others to print on demand. "On demand" means that your books are printed as they are sold, either through your website or a vendor. On demand printing services have a tendency to cost more per unit. However, you also won't be faced with dozens of boxes to store in your home if you go with bulk printing. If you have adequate storage and have more upfront to spend, it is a viable option.

EXERCISE TWENTY-NINE

1. Are you self-publishing or exploring traditional routes?

For Traditional:

1. When is the book being released?
2. How many copies are they providing you for advanced reader copies (ARCs)?
3. How much will additional copies cost for you to purchase from the publisher to sell?
4. How much profit will that net you per printed book?

For Self-Publishing:

1. Find vendors to utilize for self-publishing. Vet at least three vendors for each major process to see who provides what level of quality and for what costs. With each option, find out their estimated costs, specific skills and benefits as a vendor, and any relevant examples they can provide of their work.
   a. Copy Editors
   b. Cover Designers
   c. Proofreaders
   d. Publication Formatter
   e. Publishing Platform
2. Among the vendors, who provided the best work for the best price? Choose your top choice and alternate for each of the vendors.
3. Can you afford your top choices for each category?
4. What are the total estimated costs?

WORKSPACE

_____

_____

_____

_____

_____

_____

_____

_____

_____

_____

_____

_____

_____

_____

_____

_____

_____

_____

_____

_____

_____

_____

WEBSITE

Say hello to your second mandatory. This, like actually writing books, is not an option. We live in a digital world, welcome to it. Anyone who tells you that a website isn't mandatory likely doesn't know enough about the industry to be giving advice. Even the most established authors in the world have some sort of online presence. A website is an easy, centralized location for your author brand and available products. Another reason this is non-negotiable is because creating a website can be free. There are thousands of attractive templates available.

One area of the website that should be mandatory is a unique URL. A URL is a Unique Resource Locator; what you type in a web browser to find a website. A unique URL is catchy, easy to remember and easy to type in. If you choose a website with a free template, but do not have a unique URL, your website address will look something like this: http://webplatform.com/user/148958694. A business card, social post or table runner will look much better with ThomasAFowler.com than the nasty URL mentioned above.

URLs can be purchased a few ways. Many website platforms offer URL purchases as an add-on service. There are also domain purchase websites where you can check to see if your desired URL is available and then purchase it. Often when you purchase a URL through a domain site, you have to sync the account. However, this is quite easy as many of those domain sites will give you instructions on how to set up the URL to sync with your website platform.

The content of your website should be clean and simple. Avoid getting too verbose, as this is a marketing tool and not your writing itself. Your website is a device to point people in the direction of your writing and tell them why it is the best book for them to read right now. The website should have your major works, a page about you and connections to your social media. The homepage needs to be a direct, engaging conversation. When a person hops onto a homepage, you have seconds to get their attention. Oftentimes, people will decide within 3-7 seconds whether they're going to stay on a website or not. That is why you need dynamic imagery and a headline that catches attention. If your homepage isn't engaging, you'll see something called a "high bounce rate," which means that people who visit your site take a quick look and get out.

If the headline and design are enticing, then it's up to the remaining content to do the talking. There are several options as to what can be included. A sub-headline can support the headline as headlines are not meant to be any longer than five words. The sub-headline can clarify the catchy message you've just provided. Ideally, the headline and sub-headline will tell the visitor what the benefit of visiting the site is. It's vital that you not just say what the product is. Rather, you have to tell them why it is unique, and why it is important to them. Creative personalities have a tendency to think intrinsically. From a marketing perspective, the consumer has to understand the benefit provided to them. Once you have engaged them by providing that benefit, you can reinforce that benefit and ask for their business.

Resources on a website can include the features of your brand. If you've created unique digital experiences through an eBook, explain that. Highlight the unique selling points that separate you from everyone else. Resources can also include review quotes of your books, as well as award nominations and wins. Having well-known reviewers rave about your work is definitely helpful; people often find reviewers they like and trust, and look for the books they liked. Resources can also provide previews, links to interviews with the media or visits on other author blogs. All of this is to show the benefit of your brand and the products offered by said brand.

After resources, the website visitor has been on your site for a while. You've avoided a bounce. They have found it worth their time to read. Now the time has come to ask for a sale. This is done through a "call-to-action." The CTA is where a conversion occurs. In this instance, a CTA conversion means consumers are headed to the page to buy your book. You can provide secondary CTAs, such as blog and social media following. Those are important, but not as important as your primary goal of selling books. As a result, ensure your primary CTAs are seen instantly. Consumers should not have to scroll down or browse through the homepage to find your CTA. Secondary CTAs can go below the fold, meaning they can be found upon browsing further through the website homepage.

After the homepage is constructed, you can build additional pages. They can include feeds of your blog or social media, feature pages on specific books, and an about page telling the reader about yourself or your self-publishing house. This will be where your brand and the products and/or services will have to be catered.

EXERCISE THIRTY

1. What is the name of your website (author name is fine, don't force it if you don't have an easily shareable name in mind)?

2. Is the URL available?
   a. If yes, do you have the budget to purchase the URL ($15-20/year average)?
   b. If no, what alternate, less expensive URLs can you use that will be just as easy to share and use in your marketing?
3. What pages does your website need? (Home, Store, About, Publications, etc.)
4. What is the purpose of each page?
5. After publication of your book, do you have remaining budget for website production?
   a. If yes, how much are you willing to allocate, knowing there are multiple other options for spending budget?
      i. Will your website require extensive coding or design?
      ii. How much will your developers or designers cost?
   b. If no, choose three website platforms that are free to host. What makes them a good choice and what limitations do they have?
      i. Are there any obstacles that make you worried about your top choice?
         1. If yes, what are they and can they be overcome?
         2. If no, go with your top choice.

WORKSPACE

BLOG

Many would say this is another mandatory. The challenge with the blog will be what you have to say on your blog. Like everything else, unique content separates your blog from an oversaturated market. Without a separated message, the blog will disappear in a vast ocean of information. Whatever your brand, your blog posts need to focus on the niche you're carving for yourself, simultaneously with your brand. From there, the direction of the content will come together.

Your blog does not have to fixate on writing, nor should it. That's exceedingly exhausted. As you draft your blog, find something about your brand that can be spoken about that isn't regularly available. If you are an author in thrillers and have police experience, the real world integrated with your fiction is a great hook. As a result, sharing what you know via a blog can generate great traffic. This serves a want and need of an audience. Authors will absorb the research and create networking opportunities. Readers will want to read about your process, and thus learn more about what you have to offer.

Whatever the content, keep consistency with your post schedules. Slow and steady wins the race. Build a schedule and understand that blog posts need to be edited and proofread. Lay out topics of discussion ahead of time. Make sure you have enough time to adequately support the blog while not forgetting the primary goal of writing your books.

Once those are all aligned, begin posting on a regular basis. Be sure to engage fellow bloggers. Write guest posts and invite others to do a guest post series. Ensure your strategy brings others to the blog, and that invitations for engagement are available. Those engagements can include adding interviews and content reviews, and ensuring your posts have links to purchase your book. After all, if a blog is free, it should support the premium content that will generate revenue and create a sustainable brand for you.

For strong content that provides consistent delivery and increased impressions, there are several aspects that should be put into place: quality content, imagery, headlines, tags, organic search engine optimization, categories, and sharing functionality.

Quality Content: Don't post just to post. Everything needs to be high quality to increase loyalists to the blog. If only a third of your posts are of decent quality, people will find another blog that has consistency in their quality.

Imagery: Statistics show that visual imagery is far more engaging than words in advertising. Use captivating imagery to pull readers in, then let the writing do the talking.

Headlines: Write down headlines that you've clicked on. Ask yourself why you clicked on them. Notice what people are sharing and what those headlines are. Do they ask a question you want answered? Is it a numerical headline, indicating there's a list to follow? Does it tease a solution to something? Avoid pandering click-bait headlines like "What Happened Next Will

Shock You." It feels like the tabloid journalism equivalent of blog posting.

Tags: Tags are categorical references that help increase SEO. They can also create consistent presence on the web. Tags can include what the content is, the genre you're writing in, and tags should be keywords that will help people find you on the web. As people click on your post more, it will receive a higher ranking in search results. The higher your ranking, the earlier people will see your post as a result of your chosen tags.

Organic Search Engine Optimization: Like tags, organic Search Engine Optimization (SEO) helps people find your blog by searching in web browsers. Rather than just write a post, find ways to alter your language into search-friendly terms. For example: you do research on swords in Medieval England and write a post about it. A non-optimized article would have jumbled sentences and language where key information would be there, but not sequenced together. An optimized article would have a headline such as "What Swords Were Used in Medieval England?" This sounds like something a person would enter when searching the web. As a result, when they search, they'll start to see your article.

Categories: Categories can help visitors find specific focuses of your blog with ease. For example, let's say you do author interviews as well as articles about how doing yoga can improve your writing. Creating two categories within your blog will help people identify which category the post belongs to. That way, if someone loves your interviews but doesn't care for your posts about yoga, they can click on the "Author Interview" category and find only those articles. This helps keep you organized.

Sharing Functionality: If your blog merely exists, there will be little users can do to see new posts other than subscribe to the blog directly. Not everyone wants e-mails about every blog post. As a result, make sure your blog is connected to your social media channels. When you add a new post, blog followers won't just see it, social media followers will see it as well. This provides an easy way to share. From there, the quality content, imagery, headlines, tags, organic search engine optimization, categories, and sharing functionality will take care of the rest.

EXERCISE THIRTY-ONE

1. Will you blog?
2. What will be the primary subject of your blog content?
3. What content (or blog subjects) will be provided regularly?
4. How often will those be posted?
5. What hashtags can be utilized to allow people to find your posts via social media?
6. What search terminology will help people find your post content who don't know about your blog yet?
7. How will you categorize your content for easy content pairings?
8. What social media will you connect to your blog so that followers can see updates automatically?
9. How can you implement imagery into your blogs?
10. What are those images and how do they tie into your blog or content?

11. If you don't have specific imagery, can you use your author logo or headshot as a substitute? (If you don't have any of these, get an author headshot from a friend with a decent camera.)

WORKSPACE

SOCIAL MEDIA

A shift has been slowly occurring. As blogs and social media took off, there came a point when having a presence was necessary for submissions and queries. No social platform, not interested.

A few things came from this mandate. The first was a revelation. Followers do not automatically equal conversion. While some authors had massive numbers of subscriptions and followers, when push came to shove, that became a crutch. It was assumed there would be immediate success because "the platform was already there." The truth is, there are bestselling authors at the top of their game with only a few hundred followers, and there are starving self-publishers who have over 30,000 followers.

Use social media to connect with fellow authors, set up opportunities for events, and speak with your fan base. Do not use it just to distract from writing or make noise. Utilizing many of the rules for blog posts, social media needs some structure to follow to avoid being a spark in the middle of a bonfire.

Hashtags: Hashtags are phrases combined using # in front of it. The most common in the writing world is #amwriting. This speaks to audiences that you are writing and pursuing that as a goal. Find hashtags that already exist and are relevant to you, and which hashtags you can create and implement into your brand. Getting a hashtag to trend is incredibly difficult, and normally needs ad support to do so. Also, make sure any hashtags you use on social media aren't trademarked or the property of a company or individual. Like all creative content, don't piggyback on another author's hashtag to try to sell your book. #amwriting is fine because it's a conversation piece to find people with common interests. Replying to a big publisher and using their posts and hashtags to get attention will only sour people's perception of you, and could get your social media accounts suspended if you're flagged enough.

Content & Post Calendar: Schedule your posts regarding your marketing efforts. Add some variety to the messages being sent so that you don't send out the same five tweets about your book. Leave space for current news that you find. That way, your social media can be adaptive and responsive to latest events.

Community Identification: Find writers similar to you and follow them. Find out what they're posting, reach out for author interviews and start interacting. The larger your community, the further your reach. Think of social media as real life conversations: introducing people to one another and entering active discussions with intelligent contributions keeps the community and conversation active.

Rule of 90/10: This is a rule for social media to keep from being too intrusive. Social media is an easy platform to get incredibly selfish. Be selfless. 90% of your content shared should be someone else's. Sharing others' content helps build that community you're working to build. By keeping your own content limited to 10%, you'll avoid over-saturation. As you search other pages, you will find someone who does the opposite. They post only their own material and keep from sharing the work of others. You'll see that their favorites and re-tweet rates will decrease over time because there will be no benefit to remaining with the social media brand. Just like in real life, if all you do is talk about yourself, no one will want to talk to you.

EXERCISE THIRTY-TWO

1. What social media platforms do you already use, if any, that can help your authorship?
2. What social media platforms do you want to start using?
3. What does the platform rely on? (Are posts limited in character count, or are they image-specific platforms?)
4. What hashtags can you use that already exist to help find readers with common interests?
5. What would a hashtag be for your author platform?
6. What communities in the publishing industry, besides readers, are you trying to connect with?
7. Who are three social media "rock stars" you appreciate?
8. What makes them so good at social media?
9. How can that translate to your social media interactions?

WORKSPACE

PRINT

With websites and social media, the majority of those can be free. There are premium options you should take if possible. Printed items are tangible; skirting costs on print is difficult, if not impossible. Like everything else in advertising, when a client takes a cheaper option, it shows. Often when budgets are trimmed, it's what takes an advertising campaign from being worthy of portfolio display to just being another day's work. Decide what makes sense within your brand to implement, as well as what you can create based on your time and budget.

Business Cards: These are great for networking, and decent cards can be printed for a manageable cost. Having these handy can be key, especially as you go to writing events and meet fellow authors. Having your website and social media on them will help establish necessary connections within the industry. Then, as opportunities arise, you can capitalize.

Bookmarks: Some use bookmarks as their business card. Oftentimes bookmarks are for specific products, like a book or series, rather than the author brand. Business cards are more for the overall business approach, whereas bookmarks can focus on a specific book you're promoting at the time. If a consumer purchases one book, and you provide them with a free bookmark that advertises a different book, it can be an easy reminder of additional product offerings.

Table Promotional Materials: Many authors make regular appearances at conventions and conferences. If all you have is a stack of books, you'll disappear into the masses of vendors. As a result, promotional materials can be a visual cue to help readers get a sense of what you offer. Like all advertising, your promotional materials should be visually appealing, and the messaging concise. Convention attendees will be swarmed with vendors and there are dozens of tables. You'll have seconds to provide something that appeals to consumers. Promotional materials should be the hooks, and then you can engage consumers in conversation about (your) books.

Digital Alternatives: At conventions, many vendors only have printed books. However, conventions and specialty events can get expensive quickly. Some convention attendees won't want to pay more for the printed version of your books. Therefore, you should have something to offer for those interested in the eBook version. This can be a website they visit to purchase the book, or cards that offer a coupon for a discounted rate. Regardless, help those who are on the fence understand where your products can be found after an initial conversation.

Free Promotional Materials: How can you get your brand and products out there? There is always the S.W.A.G. (Stuff We All Get) approach. These can be items that you purchase in bulk, and give away for free to keep your name and presence felt (pens, bumper stickers, notepads, bags). Some brands provide lanyards for convention attendees. There can also be promotional giveaways. The giveaway can be your books, or a higher quality giveaway like drink ware, t-shirts or hats.

EXERCISE THIRTY-THREE

1. Does it make sense to have a traditional business card for your brand?
2. If you want something unconventional (like a business card that doubles as a beer opener, or cards that have seeds you can plant inside them), what would it be?
3. Why would that make sense for your brand?
4. How can bookmarks be designed to support your brand?
5. What would the copy be on your card and/or bookmark? (This is the most concise communication you can muster.)
    a. Who are you? (Give only your brand name and tagline.)
    b. What are you offering?
    c. Where can they get it?
6. Do you need additional promotional materials for conventions and appearances?
    a. If so, what are they?
7. What S.W.A.G. makes sense for your brand?
8. For each printed item you've chosen, reach out to three printers or vendors for costs. Don't forget the design process and cover the exact deliverable they're providing for you. Often vendors provide specifications for delivery. What are their costs? Do they provide any added benefit over the other vendors? When can you expect final delivery?

_____

_____

_____

_____

_____

_____

_____

_____

_____

_____

_____

_____

_____

_____

_____

_____

_____

_____

_____

_____

_____

_____

_____

_____

CONVENTIONS AND APPEARANCES

Regardless of genre, a key element to your brand should be appearances. The nature of said appearances will vary depending on what you write. Sci-fi, fantasy and comic book writers are perfect fits for comic conventions. There are dedicated conventions for romance writers. Literary writers will thrive at award ceremonies. This can get costly without much of a return on investment (ROI), if done improperly. Strong research and discussion with writers will be key. Knowing which awards have a tendency to provide strong awareness, and increased chance of publisher interest, are worth entry fees.

Never think that the smaller the convention, the lesser the opportunity. Larger attended cons can be great, but due to sheer volume, you can have a hard time making strong connections. Smaller conventions give you a chance for higher quality business opportunities. As a result, your appearances should have some diversity. Each convention should have key objectives. If there is a key person you want to meet and hopefully create a lasting connection, focus on that. Never turn away from a networking opportunity. At the same time, keep your appearance objectives in mind at all times. Odds are many of the attendees will have nothing for you. However, braveness will lead to reward. Remember: give and take.

If a convention is known for mass attendance, it may be a better chance to get tons of fan interactions and build your fan base. As you enter panels and scout awards, reach out to authors who have either attended the convention or entered the award in years past. What did they find beneficial? What were some of the issues? How can that information translate into the best utilization of your time?

EXERCISE THIRTY-FOUR

1. What are the biggest conventions in your genre?
2. How easy is it to secure an appearance at those conventions?
3. What smaller or regional conventions/appearances are within your genre or expertise?
4. Of the venues you've chosen, are there any table rental costs or vendor fees, or is the convention providing you space?
5. Of the venues you've chosen, what have other authors said about their average sales and return on investment (ROI) from appearing there?
6. Based on costs and anticipated ROI, which conventions make the most sense to begin with?
7. Which conventions or appearances would be considered optional with the information you have?

WORKSPACE

DIGITAL MATERIALS & CONTENT

There is more to the Internet than just a website, blog and social media. Those are items anyone can do for free, if necessary. It's always nice to support the author trifecta of requirement with creative, visual content. However, there are even more opportunities with paid digital materials and content.

Display Advertising: Display advertising are the images or banners that are on top, to the sides, and sometimes take over a website momentarily. There are a ton of options to create display advertising. Depending on where display advertising is placed, there are different specs required. At this point, display advertising can be implemented into smart televisions, video game systems and anything that relies on the web for functionality.

The easiest approach for display advertising is "static banners." These are still images with no animation implemented. One benefit is that they are simple. You get a single frame to convey every piece of information you need. This can be a challenge because you'll need a headline, a CTA, and a visual component (such as your book cover).

If the display advertising is small, it can get tough to really speak to the consumer.

Animated banners have more than one frame; normally you can allocate up to three frames. This gives you the chance to tell a grander story. However, animated banners typically are not allowed to be longer than 10 seconds. This means each of your frames will have very little time for the reader to see. With animated banners, make sure that your final frame can be independent; animated banners do not loop. Also, with the benefit of multiple frames comes a new challenge: coding.

Animated banners required HTML5 coding. There are web platforms to help you develop banners yourself, if you feel challenged. However, if you wish to create truly great display advertising, you'll need some design help and coding to make sure you can properly monitor and track your conversions on banners. Without tracking, you won't have the information about who's clicked the banners and how they inteacted with them.

The next step can also include dynamic creative display advertising. These are ads that can be adjusted and modified depending on a number of variables. You can create messaging that is tailored to specific times; you can adjust banners for temporary sales promotions. This is beneficial as you can adjust based on numbers and interactions. However, you will see added challenges with knowing how display advertising ad serving platforms work, and how to code the display to work properly. As a result, these will cost more as you'll likely need the assistance of a developer to create the banners.

Another consideration is how small the margins are for display advertising success. If 1% of people who see your display advertising click on the banner, you're doing great. For every 1,000 users who see your ad, you may enjoy 10 clicks. As a result, you'll be paying for a ton of people to see the ad, but very few will do a thing about it. There is a place for display advertising, and with a strong CTA, your conversions can work well. In addition, many ad-serving platforms allow for targeted display. Then, if the statistics show a certain leniency toward a specific banner, you can increase the amount of rotation those ads receive, allowing your more successful ad to show more often.

More advanced placements, such as expanding banners and takeovers, are the types of display advertising that can become annoying. Visit the sites you're thinking about advertising on and make sure their approach isn't too encroaching on the user. If it is intrusive, or they have too many offers on a single page, this is one of the quickest routes to a fast bounce rate. See what the site has, how it's put into layout and what advertising they're showing currently.

Native Advertising: This has become incredibly popular over the last few years. However, with great popularity comes great cost. You may not realize you're seeing native advertising. They can be as simple as articles or lists on popular websites.

Native advertising is not a direct ad. Rather, it is often content relevant to the company or product. Then, somewhere within the page will be an element to help visitors engage the brand. This can come with a closing statement like "This article was brought to you by..." or an opening statement like "23 Valentine's Day DIY Hacks, Courtesy of Author J.B. Smith." Somewhere, there will be an opportunity to sell the product. If you're unsure about the success of native advertising, you can often request case studies about their typical statistics from sponsored content. Many native advertising platforms also have sales reps who can help you find the right content to sponsor.

Paid Search: Organic search is when you write an article or post that has terms within it that people will naturally look for. Then, when they search for the specific term embedded within your text, they find your article. Paid search is when you are actually paying money to show up in search results. It is always indicated if your search is paid for.

Paid search is a fine line because broad terms like "Great New Book" will cost a lot. Many people want that search term for their writing, and rightfully so. It's a competitive space. On the flip side, "Murder Mystery Novel Family Conspiracy" may specifically discuss your book. However, it may not be searched enough to make an impact. The perfect balance may be "Conspiracy Murder Mystery."
You can often analyze the trends as you build a search campaign. It's often better if you have multiple paid search pieces on the web. Then, depending on the results, you can adjust your advertising in real time. You always want to provide 2-3 weeks at a minimum to see how effective your advertising is.

Video: Video content finds better engagement than many of the other listed digital approaches. However, video can be an incredible hindrance. Poor video production quality shows, and it shows fast. While there are plenty of editing programs in the market, many introductory level programs offer basic functions. Advanced editing programs with the capacity for motion graphics or animation require extensive knowledge to execute properly.

Therefore, it's vital to select the right strategy for your video content in branding. If you have resources to create more dramatic pieces with careful edits, then fewer high quality videos could be the way to go. If you want videos to support your blog with quickly shot vlogs, go for it. It really boils down to what your brand, budget and timing are all capable of supporting. Watch book trailers, vlogs, interviews with other authors and your favorite channels. Take the time to understand what went into the actual creation of them. You can always reach out to authors and ask them where they found their resources. Nothing helps business more than networking opportunities. Many video editors and graphic artists live or die by references.

Simultaneously, you can find a cheaper, more consistent presence via videos shot at home with quick messages to your readers and dedicated audience members. Tell a concise story with your videos. These should be pieces of communication with the notion of further engagement. A book trailer should have enough to intrigue viewers, but leave them wanting. Vlogs posted on social media should be quick engagements to convey a message or something to benefit the viewer. Like your brand, without understanding the mission statement, the videos will fall flat. First define why the video content has to exist, then you can know how to create the content.

One way to identify production costs ahead of time is from script and storyboard creation. Storyboards are a visual guide as to how videos will be made. If you're researching outside vendors, storyboards will help editors create accurate estimates for production. They also ensure the vision of the video is translated accurately when it enters production. If you decide on simply doing video interviews or vlogs, storyboarding would be excessive. In those cases, a solid script is all you'll need.

EXERCISE THIRTY-FIVE

1. Do you have the capacity to create digital display advertising banners?
2. Will they be static images or animated banners?
3. What ad delivery platform will they be served through?
4. What targeting information can you set up to optimize delivery and ensure you're reaching the right audience?

5. What is the content of said display advertisements?

6. What sites do you visit, that reach your target audience, that makes sense for native advertising?

7. Do those sites offer case studies on the average ROI of crating native advertising with those sites?

8. How much will it cost to produce?

9. What terms would you use for paid searches to heighten your page results in web browsers?

10. Do you have any budget remaining for paid search?

11. Is it enough to truly make an impact, remembering that display advertising and paid search results have very low engagement numbers? Thousands of impressions will result in only a few conversions or sales.

12. Do you have the budget for video? If so, what is it?

13. What is the content of the video for your brand?

14. Who will be filming, editing, and finalizing your videos?

15. Are there any talent costs? If so, how many do you anticipate and what level of talent can you afford?

16. Can you film video brand content with a guerrilla approach, or does your brand require full, high-quality video production?

17. What music and sound effects are required? Where are they coming from? Do you have a post-production specialist available or will you need a recording studio to provide assets?

18. Do you only have the budget for stock audio from a royalty-free site?

19. What variable assets are required for your video or any of the digital content production areas?

WORKSPACE

SPONSORSHIP

S ponsorship is everywhere, and is when you assist another brand in achieving something. This can be a specific product, helping to make an event occur, or even covering production costs for something. When you hear the phrase "Brought to you by..." or "This episode of the podcast was made possible thanks to..." that is sponsorship. It, in a way, is a paid endorsement of another product. In turn, you are provided sponsorship advertising that endorses your product.

Find local events you can help sponsor. Any podcasts, radio, or websites that could tie into your books and brand can be potential sponsorship opportunities. Much larger sponsorship venues and opportunities can provide case studies and metrics, proving what sponsorship averages in terms of return. It can provide details as to how many people listen to a specific show you may want to sponsor and how many people attend an event.

You should also investigate whether the sponsorship is the right fit. Make sure the target demographics identified previously engage the brand, event or product you are sponsoring. Eventually, your brand could become large enough that others will want to sponsor you. Take the opportunity and make sure there is a return on the investment for the sponsor. You'll want that when you're the one paying for a sponsorship, so provide that same benefit.

EXERCISE THIRTY-SIX

1. List five websites, podcasts, events or videos you could sponsor.
2. Why do these sites make sense for your brand to sponsor?
3. What are their respective sponsorship costs?
4. What level of engagement does each of the five see with an average sponsorship? (If they cannot provide that information, the sponsorship had better be dirt cheap, because that means they're either just starting out or don't measure their success. The latter is a red flag.)
5. Based on the sponsorship case studies and engagement statistics, will the sponsorships provide viable ROI?

WORKSPACE

FINAL PRODUCTION PLAN

N ow that the list of prioritized items has been made, it's time to see how much you anticipate spending and adjust. It's likely you'll have to remove an item you wanted. Continue revising the list of production materials for your brand until you reach the time and dollar amount you have to allocate to your brand. Place removed items on the back-burner. As you generate revenue from your brand, you could allocate additional dollars to new advertising. As well, when you receive data and results from your advertising, you can shift your spending to advertising that does work. There's a reason there isn't a singular answer.

EXERCISE THIRTY-SEVEN

Before executing all of the things you selected and chose for your brand production, it's time for a budget analysis. Can you execute everything you said you could?

1. What was your total budget?

2. What are the total costs of all the production elements you decided on?

3. Take that number and add a 15% contingency for miscellaneous costs (such as travel expenses to conventions, taxes, meals, expedited shipping, etc.). If you are fiscally conservative and worry, go to 20% contingency.

4. What are your total estimated costs of production?

5. Are you within budget?

6. If so, congratulations and get started!

7. If not, what executions can you remove? Start with your least required production element and keep cutting until you hit that target budget. Remember, you can always use revenue to add to future production budgets.

WORKSPACE

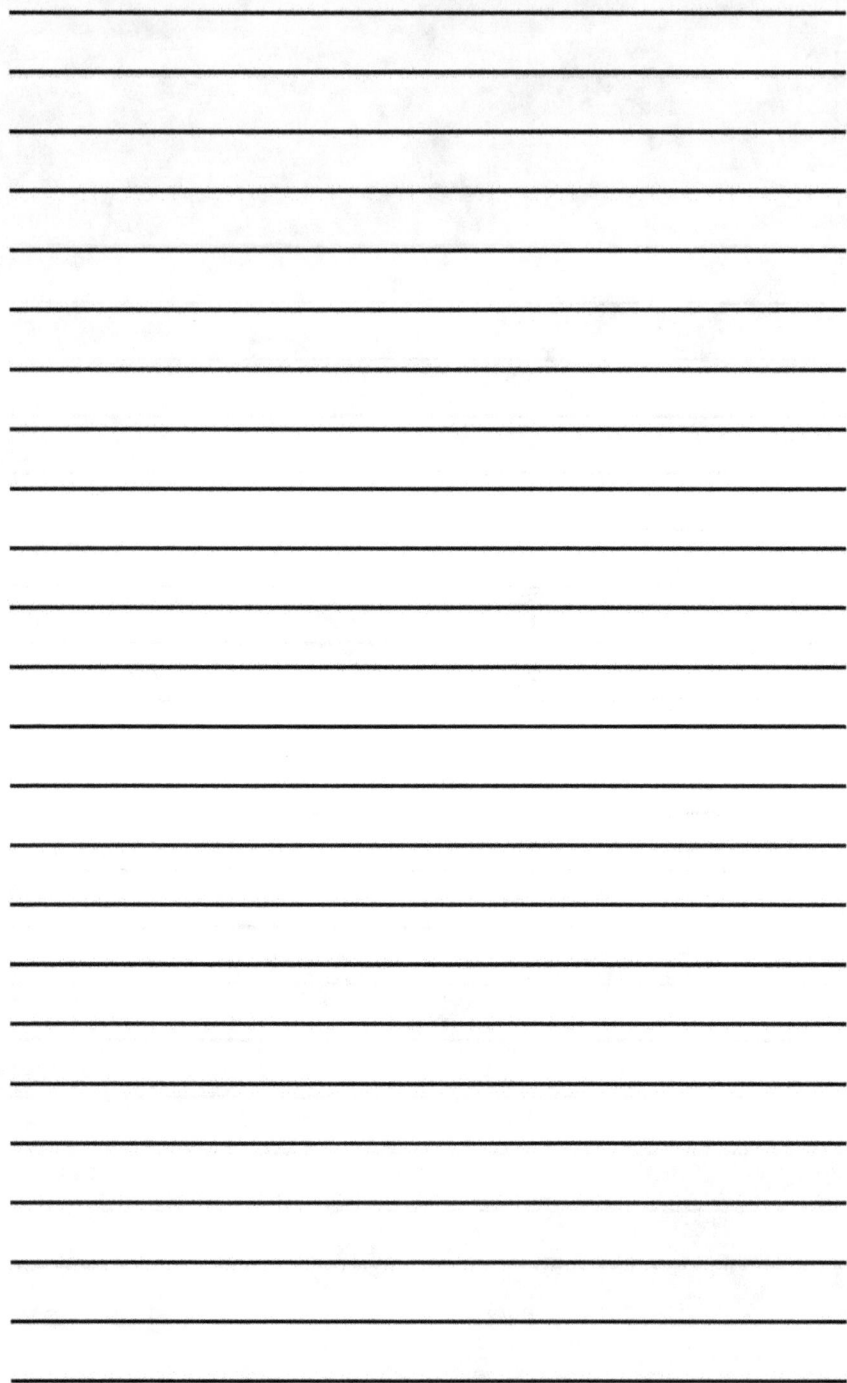

CONCLUSION

A s your brand hits the market, give it time before making drastic decisions. Brands take time to build. Understand mistakes will happen. You are no longer aspiring or saying "someday." With each mistake, your brand will adapt into something new and stronger.

Get to work, release your brand to the world. Take pride in the work you put in to making this a reality. You will find criticism; you will see some disappointing results at times. With those hurdles also comes success. One day you will introduce yourself at an event, and you'll introduce yourself seamlessly. The words will pour out; people will know exactly what you write, and what your author voice sounds like. When that moment comes, it means your brand is established. Once that occurs, it'll be time to see what should remain to keep the brand voice present to the now loyal fan base, and what can be created to further your career through additional, successful marketing efforts to support your incredible books.

Congratulations on making it through this book. The research and amount of exercises you endured is staggering. Hopefully, you now have all the tools to launch your brand into the market and make a true impact in the right way.

No one takes that away from you. You are a unique voice to enter the market.

It is your book; it is your brand.

INDEX

Analytics: A reporting tool that provides data regarding how web, mobile, and tablet device users are interacting with your website.

App: An application developed for operating systems that allow for specific interactions by a user. Most often provided for mobile and tablet devices. App development can include such categories as gaming, niche fan interactions, utilities and social media.

Appearances: Public events in which you, the author, are profiled and allowed to be at an event for a specific purpose, which can lead to new leads, social media engagement and potential sales.

Attachment: When consumers begin to not only understand what your brand has to offer, but engage it and begin finding a benefit in utilizing your brand specifically.

Awareness: An early brand strategy aimed at making consumers aware of what your brand is and, more importantly, what it has to offer.

Background Reasoning: The historical reference as to why your brand should exist and why it has a viable place in the market.

Banner: A method of display advertising, banners can be static images or animated advertisements placed on websites to advertise to potential consumers.

Blog: A website or web page that provides consistent content, often through a more informal style that mimics conversation or casual education. Often focused with specific niches in mind.

Bounce Rate: A calculation of how many people arrive on a website, but leave before exploring any other pages. If multiple users go to your homepage, but do not go to your store or about page, then you have a high bounce rate. If users often explore multiple pages on your website and don't leave after viewing a single page, you have a low bounce rate. Calculate your rate with this formula: Visits with only 1 page view / Total Visits = Bounce Rate.

Brand: A specifically named organization offering a particular product or service.

Brand Goals: Specific aims for your brand at a particular juncture, which may change over time as your brand expands and achieves particular goals.

Brand Objective(s): Broad aspirations regarding how you want consumers to perceive the products offered.

Brand Positioning Statement: A concise, deliberate version of a particular mission statement for a brand.

Brand Strategy: A carefully constructed series of approaches to your advertising to fulfill specific goals and objectives.

Brief: A summary of the key goals for a brand or campaign that are to be achieved in order to guide advertising efforts.

Budget: The total amount of available funds for your business to operate.

Call to Action (CTA): Typically at the end of an advertising experience, the CTA is the guidance to a potential consumer as to how they can engage your brand. ("Pre-Order Now," "Subscribe Here," etc.)

Category: The specific business market in which a brand is entering and attempting to sell products or services.

Click Bait: A headline intentionally written to lure web users in to sharing or clicking on a specific article using faux pas or emotionally manipulative text.

Code: Lines of information entered to construct websites, applications and software, and communicate with devices as to how they are to see the developed elements of the code.

Conventions (Cons): Large events for specific fanbases and audiences featuring artists and performers that work within the categories of the convention itself.

Conversion Rates: These are calculations based on how many people are following your call to action. If that goal is to sell books, then a good conversion rate would occur when you have an advertisement and multiple people click on it, and then purchase your book because of the engagement that started because of said advertisement.

Conversions: When a consumer engages your brand to fulfill a specific brand goal.

Cost Per Acquisition (CPA): The amount of money it takes to spend on your advertising to get people to engage your brand. If it takes more money to acquire a costumer than the product is worth, the CPA is a loss. Calculate your cost per acquisition with the following formula: Amount of money spent on advertising / Number of books sold from advertising = Cost Per Acquisition.

Cost Per Impression (CPM): The amount of money spent in order to have a specific amount of people see your advertisements. The numbers are often calculated per 1,000 people. A CPM of $35 means it costs $35 for 1,000 people to see your advertisement. CPM does not guarantee engagement, it merely guarantees an impression.

Delivery: The methods in which consumers receive your brand product or service, which helps define brand voice and personality based on the methods chosen.

Display Advertising: Visual digital advertising that gives an image, supported by headlines and a call to action, allowing users to understand what you offer and how they can acquire it.

Dynamic Creative: Advanced digital placements that allow for more advanced features beyond impressions and clicks including, but not limited to, responsive text customization, expandable features and video integration.

Differentiation: The method in which your brand will separate itself from the competition within the category and market in which it resides.

eBook: A digital publication of a book that is used with a device including, but not limited to, mobile phones, tablets and eReaders.

E-mail: A direct electronic message sent to specific addresses. E-mail subscribers receive content curated and sent by your brand to further engage the brand.

Emotion: The catharsis experience by consumers because they used your brand product or services.

Event: A specific moment or gathering in which you can promote your brand, products and/or services with specific audiences in attendance.

Experience: The way consumers would describe what using your brand is like, be it sophisticated, comedic or advanced. The brand experience guides them to know what they are being provided, and more importantly how to communicate what the experience was like.

Font: A brand element to include in marketing materials, a font is the text style and treatment that helps personify your brand.

Followers: Users on social media who decide to monitor all of your posts.

Headline: A short, enticing sentence meant to draw consumers to engage your brand.

Impression: When an interactive user sees an advertisement on a website or page.

Insistence: A final step in brand strategy, when someone using your brand refuses to engage other brands with comparable products or services.

Key Performance Indicator (KPI): A tangible measurement for which an organization or business deems success.

Logo: A visual identifier that is consistently seen on all of your advertisement efforts to help consumers recognize your brand.

Measurements: Methods in which your advertisement performances are calculated to gauge successes and challenges.

Messaging: Key words and emotional phrases that convey the intention of an advertising brand.

Native Advertising: A variation of sponsorship in which articles on popular websites are provided by a brand. Articles are often subjects or editorials in connection to elements the brand provides.

Newsletter: Either a printed or digital series of articles and notifications to a group of selected subscribers who elected to engage and receive updates.

Optimization: Reviewing the performance of your advertisements and modifying their methods of delivery to improve engagement and visibility.

Page Views: The number of times a specific part of your website is viewed by any type of user.

Pay Per Click: Advertising in which you pay every time a user engages your advertisement to go to a designated URL.

Personality: Traits of a brand that relate to the consumer as to the emotional experience a brand provides.

P.E.S.T.: An assessment of the political, economic, social and technological aspects of the market you are entering, to determine the market environment.

Pre-Production: The process of planning the actual creation of your brand and products including budgeting, vendor outreach, estimated timeframes for delivery and anticipated costs.

Press Release: A public notification sent to news outlets and media to inform of a major event or release.

Print: Advertising using traditional printing methods for elements such as business cards, banners, bookmarks and additional promotional items.

Production: The period in which products and advertisements are being made.

Production Parameters: Specifications and methods for delivery that determine rules for how a particular advertisement or product is made.

Promotion: An activity or advertisement that entices engagement with a brand to gain additional purchases.

Rationale: A written background to justify the approach of a brand and why it will appeal to consumers.

Recognition: The first step of strategy for a new brand, the advertising aims to make consumers understand what your brand is and what it has to offer.

Reporting: Consolidated documents covering the performance of your brand and its advertising.

Responsive: A website or page that can understand the device being used and adjust the fonts, imagery and layout to display properly.

Retention: Keeping consumers engaged with your brand.

Return on Investment (ROI): How much money advertisements brought in, and calculating whether it was a viable return.

SEO (Organic): Text placed on websites and blog posts that users commonly enter when searching for products your brand offers, allowing them to naturally find your brand.

SEO (Paid): Paying a company to promote your website pages for a higher spot on search results when users look for specific phrases on a search engine.

Sponsorship: Paying for a brand to create an event or promotion by profiling sponsors as a means of raising awareness for those sponsoring the event or promotion.

Social Engagement: Interactions from users who like, follow or respond to posts of yours.

Social Media: Applications and websites in which users create and share content or updates to a group of followers.

Sub-Headline: A more detailed sentence providing additional information beyond a headline, to further entice consumers to engage the brand.

Subscribers: Consumers who elect to receive curated content from your brand either via direct e-mail, newsletters or social media.

S.W.O.T.: An assessment of your brand strengths, weaknesses, opportunities and threats to gauge what your brand has to offer in the market and how it can communicate through advertising.

Tagline: A brief phrase used to pair with a brand logo and its advertising that identifies what is offered and how it can emotionally resonate with consumers.

Target Audience & Demographics: Specific elements of consumers who are likely to engage your brand and purchase your products.

Tone: A method of speech that provides a personality to consumers, letting them know what emotional experience they will be provided should they engage your brand.

Trafficking: Sending advertising materials to vendors, all set to exact specifications.

Unique Visitors: The number of interactive users that visit your website. This provides the number of people visiting your site, as opposed to page views that shows how many times your site has been seen.

Uniform Resource Location (URL): A unique address on the internet allowing files to be viewed and accessed, most often a website.

User Interface (UI): In web development specifically, UI is defined by how the average consumer will interact with the website, and what those interactions do.

User Experience (UX): Going beyond what the interactions are, the experience defines how the digital interactions will feel to the user and how the movement through the website is made as effortless as possible.

Video: Visual advertisements that go beyond the written word for promotion.

Voice: Consistent communication with advertising that exemplifies the brand personality.

Webinar: A digital gathering to teach or interact with others via video, instant messaging conversations, and QA sessions.

Website: A specific location on the internet allowing for the communication of information to those visiting said location, and to provide consumers with what the brand is and why they should engage its product and/or services.

Wireframes: A basic layout with no design, copy or major functionality entered into the code of a website, to plan the structure of your website.

Wrap Report: At the end of a promotional period or advertising campaign, a wrap report summarizes analytics and other statistical data about what worked, what didn't and how the brand can adjust to succeed in future promotions and campaigns.

ABOUT THE AUTHOR

Thomas A. Fowler is the author of nerdy things. By day he works as a Broadcast & Digital Producer at a full-service ad agency in Denver, Colorado. Campaigns he's served as producer on have been featured on *AdWeek, Creativity*, and *The Denver Egotist*. He has worked on campaigns that have won at The Fifty, as well as the Business Marketing Association's Gold Key Award.

By night, Thomas is a writer of commercial mainstream and science fiction. His short stories have been published by RuneWright Publishing & Story of the Month Club. He was the writer of the feature film *The Code: Legend of the Gamers*, which screened at film festivals and is available for streaming on IMDb. His screenplay *Dreams of Exile* was a film-festival finalist for Best Original Screenplay at the Paranoia Horror Film Festival.

Thomas is blissfully married to Amber, a beautiful woman way out of his league. He also has two gorgeous daughters, Emma and Grace, who challenge him to be a better man each and every day.

*Learn more about Fowler at his website,
ThomasAFowler.com. He is also active on Twitter and
Facebook, feeding the proverbial social machine.*

www.ingramcontent.com/pod-product-compliance
Lightning Source LLC
Chambersburg PA
CBHW030934220326
41521CB00040B/2323